한국어(Korean)

동사(verb) 290

형용사(adjective) 137

English(영어)
translation(번역판)

< 저자(author) >

㈜한글2119연구소

· 연구개발전담부서

· ISO 9001 : 품질경영시스템 인증

· ISO 14001 : 환경경영시스템 인증

· 이메일(e-mail) : gjh0675@naver.com

< 동영상(video) 자료(material) >

HANPUK_english(translation)
https://www.youtube.com/@HANPUK_English

제 2024153361 호

연구개발전담부서 인정서

1. 전담부서명: 연구개발전담부서

   [소속기업명: (주)한글2119연구소]

2. 소 재 지: 인천광역시 부평구 마장로264번길 33
   상가동 제지하층 제2호 (산곡동, 뉴서울아파트)

3. 신고 연월일: 2024년 05월 02일

과학기술정보통신부

「기초연구진흥 및 기술개발지원에 관한 법률」 제14조의
2제1항 및 같은 법 시행령 제27조제1항에 따라 위와 같이
기업의 연구개발전담부서로 인정합니다.

2024년 5월 13일

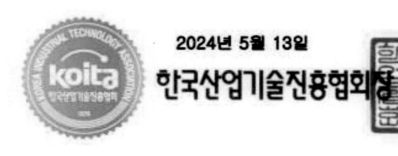

한국산업기술진흥협회장

G-CERTI *Certificate*

hereby certifies that

Hangul 2119 Research Institute Co., Ltd.

Rm. 2, Lower level, Sangga-dong, 33, Majang-ro 264beon-gil, Bupyeong-gu, Incheon, Korea

meets the Standard Requirements & Scope as following

ISO 9001:2015
Quality Management Systems

**Creation of Media Content, Publication
of Korean Paper and Electronic Textbooks, Production
and Release of Albums for Korean Language Education**

Certificate No: GIS-6934-QC	**Code**	: 08, 39
Initial Date : 2024-05-21	**Issue Date**	: 2024-05-21
Expiry Date : 2027-05-20	**Valid Period**	: 2024-05-21 ~ 2027-05-20

Signed for and on behalf of GCERTI
President I.K. Cho

G-CERTi
SYSTEM SERVICE
MSCB-113

IAS ACCREDITED
Management Systems
Certification Body
MSCB-113

G-CERTI *Certificate*

hereby certifies that

Hangul 2119 Research Institute Co., Ltd.

Rm. 2, Lower level, Sangga-dong, 33, Majang-ro 264beon-gil,
Bupyeong-gu, Incheon, Korea

meets the Standard Requirements & Scope as following

ISO 14001:2015
Environmental Management Systems

Creation of Media Content, Publication
of Korean Paper and Electronic Textbooks, Production and
Release of Albums for Korean Language Education

Certificate No: GIS-6934-EC	Code	: 08, 39
Initial Date : 2024-05-21	Issue Date	: 2024-05-21
Expiry Date : 2027-05-20	Valid Period	: 2024-05-21 ~ 2027-05-20

Signed for and on behalf of GCERTI
President I.K.Cho

MSCB-113

< 목차(table of contents) >

한국어(Korean)

동사(verb) 290

(1) 들리다 [deullida]

be heard; be audible

For a sound to be heard and recognized through one's ears.

past : 들리 + 었어요 → 들렸어요
present : 들리 + 어요 → 들려요
future : 들리 + ㄹ 거예요 → 들릴 거예요

(2) 메다 [meda]

shoulder; carry on one's shoulder

To put something on or over one's shoulder or back.

past : 메 + 었어요 → 멨어요
present : 메 + 어요 → 메요
future : 메 + ㄹ 거예요 → 멜 거예요

(3) 보이다 [boida]

be viewed; be visible; be in sight

To come to know the presence or outward appearance of an object by looking at it.

past : 보이 + 었어요 → 보였어요
present : 보이 + 어요 → 보여요
future : 보이 + ㄹ 거예요 → 보일 거예요

(4) 귀여워하다 [gwiyeowohada]

love; make a pet of; be affectionate to

To treat a younger person or animal with affection.

past : 귀여워하 + 였어요 → 귀여워했어요
present : 귀여워하 + 여요 → 귀여워해요
future : 귀여워하 + ㄹ 거예요 → 귀여워할 거예요

(5) 기뻐하다 [gippeohada]

be glad; be happy

To be joyful and happy.

past : 기뻐하 + 였어요 → **기뻐했어요**
present : 기뻐하 + 여요 → **기뻐해요**
future : 기뻐하 + ㄹ 거예요 → **기뻐할 거예요**

(6) 놀라다 [nollada]

be surprised; be astonished; be shocked; be scared

To become tense or feel one's heart pounding as one faces an unexpected incident or is scared.

past : 놀라 + 았어요 → **놀랐어요**
present : 놀라 + 아요 → **놀라요**
future : 놀라 + ㄹ 거예요 → **놀랄 거예요**

(7) 느끼다 [neukkida]

feel

To perceive a certain stimulus through a sensory organ such as the nose, skin, etc.

past : 느끼 + 었어요 → **느꼈어요**
present : 느끼 + 어요 → **느껴요**
future : 느끼 + ㄹ 거예요 → **느낄 거예요**

(8) 슬퍼하다 [seulpeohada]

be sad

To consider as sad and sorrowful enough to cry.

past : 슬퍼하 + 였어요 → **슬퍼했어요**
present : 슬퍼하 + 여요 → **슬퍼해요**
future : 슬퍼하 + ㄹ 거예요 → **슬퍼할 거예요**

(9) 싫어하다 [sireohada]
hate; dislike
To not like or want something.

past : 싫어하 + 였어요 → **싫어했어요**
present : 싫어하 + 여요 → **싫어해요**
future : 싫어하 + ㄹ 거예요 → **싫어할 거예요**

(10) 안되다 [andoeda]
fail; not go well; be unlucky
For an affair or phenomenon to not take place properly.

past : 안되 + 었어요 → **안됐어요**
present : 안되 + 어요 → **안돼요**
future : 안되 + ㄹ 거예요 → **안될 거예요**

(11) 좋아하다 [joahada]
like
To have good feelings toward something.

past : 좋아하 + 였어요 → **좋아했어요**
present : 좋아하 + 여요 → **좋아해요**
future : 좋아하 + ㄹ 거예요 → **좋아할 거예요**

(12) 즐거워하다 [jeulgeowohada]
be pleased; be delighted
To be pleased and satisfied with something.

past : 즐거워하 + 였어요 → **즐거워했어요**
present : 즐거워하 + 여요 → **즐거워해요**
future : 즐거워하 + ㄹ 거예요 → **즐거워할 거예요**

(13) 화나다 [hwanada]

get angry; be furious; be enraged

To feel bad, being extremely upset or unhappy.

past : 화나 + 았어요 → **화났어요**
present : 화나 + 아요 → **화나요**
future : 화나 + ㄹ 거예요 → **화날 거예요**

(14) 화내다 [hwanaeda]

get angry with; be mad at

To show anger toward another, being upset with him/her.

past : 화내 + 었어요 → **화냈어요**
present : 화내 + 어요 → **화내요**
future : 화내 + ㄹ 거예요 → **화낼 거예요**

(15) 자랑하다 [jaranghada]

boast; brag; make a boast of

To say things about oneself or people or things related to oneself in order to show off.

past : 자랑하 + 였어요 → **자랑했어요**
present : 자랑하 + 여요 → **자랑해요**
future : 자랑하 + ㄹ 거예요 → **자랑할 거예요**

(16) 조심하다 [josimhada]

practice caution

To be careful in speech, behavior, etc., not to get in trouble.

past : 조심하 + 였어요 → **조심했어요**
present : 조심하 + 여요 → **조심해요**
future : 조심하 + ㄹ 거예요 → **조심할 거예요**

(17) 늙다 [neukda]

become old; age

To become very old.

past : 늙 + 었어요 → 늙었어요
present : 늙 + 어요 → 늙어요
future : 늙 + 을 거예요 → 늙을 거예요

(18) 못생기다 [motsaenggida]

ugly-looking; homely

Being below the average in terms of appearance.

past : 못생기 + 었어요 → 못생겼어요
present : 못생기 + 어요 → 못생겨요
future : 못생기 + ㄹ 거예요 → 못생길 거예요

(19) 빼다 [ppaeda]

lose; remove

To reduce fat, weight, etc.

past : 빼 + 었어요 → 뺐어요
present : 빼 + 어요 → 빼요
future : 빼 + ㄹ 거예요 → 뺄 거예요

(20) 잘생기다 [jalsaenggida]

good-looking; handsome; comely

Having a pleasing and attractive appearance.

past : 잘생기 + 었어요 → 잘생겼어요
present : 잘생기 + 어요 → 잘생겨요
future : 잘생기 + ㄹ 거예요 → 잘생길 거예요

(21) 찌다 [jjida]

gain weight

To put more flesh on one's body and become fat.

past : 찌 + 었어요 → 쪘어요
present : 찌 + 어요 → 쪄요
future : 찌 + ㄹ 거예요 → 찔 거예요

(22) 못하다 [motada]

be incapable; fail to

To fail to make a certain work reach a certain level or to not own the ability to do so.

past : 못하 + 였어요 → 못했어요
present : 못하 + 여요 → 못해요
future : 못하 + ㄹ 거예요 → 못할 거예요

(23) 잘못하다 [jalmotada]

commit an error; blunder; misdo

To do something in an incorrect or unrighteous way.

past : 잘못하 + 였어요 → 잘못했어요
present : 잘못하 + 여요 → 잘못해요
future : 잘못하 + ㄹ 거예요 → 잘못할 거예요

(24) 잘하다 [jalhada]

do a right thing; do right

To do in a right and honest way.

past : 잘하 + 였어요 → 잘했어요
present : 잘하 + 여요 → 잘해요
future : 잘하 + ㄹ 거예요 → 잘할 거예요

(25) 가다 [gada]

go; travel

To move from one place to another place.

past : 가 + 았어요 → 갔어요
present : 가 + 아요 → 가요
future : 가 + ㄹ 거예요 → 갈 거예요

(26) 가리키다 [garikida]

point; gesture; indicate

To point a finger or some other thing in a certain direction or toward a certain object to let others recognize it.

past : 가리키 + 었어요 → 가리켰어요
present : 가리키 + 어요 → 가리켜요
future : 가리키 + ㄹ 거예요 → 가리킬 거예요

(27) 감다 [gamda]

wash; bathe

To wash one's hair or body with water.

past : 감 + 았어요 → 감았어요
present : 감 + 아요 → 감아요
future : 감 + 을 거예요 → 감을 거예요

(28) 걷다 [geotda]

walk

To lift one's feet, one foot at a time, from the ground and change their positions.

past : 걷 + 었어요 → 걸었어요
present : 걷 + 어요 → 걸어요
future : 걷 + 을 거예요 → 걸을 거예요

(29) 걸어가다 [georeogada]

walk; tread; stride

To take a step forward in the direction of a destination.

past : 걸어가 + 았어요 → 걸어갔어요
present : 걸어가 + 아요 → 걸어가요
future : 걸어가 + ㄹ 거예요 → 걸어갈 거예요

(30) 걸어오다 [georeooda]

walk; come on foot

To take a step forward in the direction of a destination.

past : 걸어오 + 았어요 → 걸어왔어요
present : 걸어오 + 아요 → 걸어와요
future : 걸어오 + ㄹ 거예요 → 걸어올 거예요

(31) 꺼내다 [kkeonaeda]

take out; carry out

To take out an object that is inside.

past : 꺼내 + 었어요 → 꺼냈어요
present : 꺼내 + 어요 → 꺼내요
future : 꺼내 + ㄹ 거예요 → 꺼낼 거예요

(32) 나오다 [naoda]

come out; get out

To come out.

past : 나오 + 았어요 → 나왔어요
present : 나오 + 아요 → 나와요
future : 나오 + ㄹ 거예요 → 나올 거예요

(33) 내려가다 [naeryeogada]

go down; step down; descend

To move from up to down.

past : 내려가 + 았어요 → 내려갔어요
present : 내려가 + 아요 → 내려가요
future : 내려가 + ㄹ 거예요 → 내려갈 거예요

(34) 내려오다 [naeryeoooda]

step down

To come from a high place to a lower place, or from up to down.

past : 내려오 + 았어요 → 내려왔어요
present : 내려오 + 아요 → 내려와요
future : 내려오 + ㄹ 거예요 → 내려올 거예요

(35) 넘어지다 [neomeojida]

fall down; trip over; tumble over

For a standing person or object to lose balance and fall down.

past : 넘어지 + 었어요 → 넘어졌어요
present : 넘어지 + 어요 → 넘어져요
future : 넘어지 + ㄹ 거예요 → 넘어질 거예요

(36) 넣다 [neota]

put; insert

To cause to go into a certain space.

past : 넣 + 었어요 → 넣었어요
present : 넣 + 어요 → 넣어요
future : 넣 + 을 거예요 → 넣을 거예요

(37) 놓다 [nota]

let go; let loose

To let something that one is either holding in one's hand or pushing be released by opening or relaxing one's hand.

past : 놓 + 았어요 → 놓았어요
present : 놓 + 아요 → 놓아요
future : 놓 + 을 거예요 → 놓을 거예요

(38) 누르다 [nureuda]

press; push

To apply one's weight to the whole or a part of an object by applying force from top to bottom.

past : 누르 + 었어요 → 눌렀어요
present : 누르 + 어요 → 눌러요
future : 누르 + ㄹ 거예요 → 누를 거예요

(39) 달리다 [dallida]

run

To come or go quickly by running.

past : 달리 + 었어요 → 달렸어요
present : 달리 + 어요 → 달려요
future : 달리 + ㄹ 거예요 → 달릴 거예요

(40) 던지다 [deonjida]

throw

To move one's arm and throw the object in one's hand in the air.

past : 던지 + 었어요 → 던졌어요
present : 던지 + 어요 → 던져요
future : 던지 + ㄹ 거예요 → 던질 거예요

(41) 돌리다 [dollida]

turn; spin

To make something move in a circle.

past : 돌리 + 었어요 → 돌렸어요
present : 돌리 + 어요 → 돌려요
future : 돌리 + ㄹ 거예요 → 돌릴 거예요

(42) 듣다 [deutda]

hear

To sense a sound with ears.

past : 듣 + 었어요 → 들었어요
present : 듣 + 어요 → 들어요
future : 듣 + 을 거예요 → 들을 거예요

(43) 들어가다 [deureogada]

enter; go into

To go inside from outside.

past : 들어가 + 았어요 → 들어갔어요
present : 들어가 + 아요 → 들어가요
future : 들어가 + ㄹ 거예요 → 들어갈 거예요

(44) 들어오다 [deureooda]

come in; get in; enter

To move inside from outside within a certain range.

past : 들어오 + 았어요 → 들어왔어요
present : 들어오 + 아요 → 들어와요
future : 들어오 + ㄹ 거예요 → 들어올 거예요

(45) 뛰다 [ttwida]

run; race; dash

To move forward in quick steps.

past : 뛰 + 었어요 → 뛰었어요
present : 뛰 + 어요 → 뛰어요
future : 뛰 + ㄹ 거예요 → 뛸 거예요

(46) 뛰어가다 [ttwieogada]

run; go running

To run and go to a certain place very fast.

past : 뛰어가 + 았어요 → 뛰어갔어요
present : 뛰어가 + 아요 → 뛰어가요
future : 뛰어가 + ㄹ 거예요 → 뛰어갈 거예요

(47) 뜨다 [tteuda]

open

To open one's closed eyes.

past : 뜨 + 었어요 → 떴어요
present : 뜨 + 어요 → 떠요
future : 뜨 + ㄹ 거예요 → 뜰 거예요

(48) 만지다 [manjida]

touch

To put one's hand on something and move it.

past : 만지 + 었어요 → 만졌어요
present : 만지 + 어요 → 만져요
future : 만지 + ㄹ 거예요 → 만질 거예요

(49) 미끄러지다 [mikkeureojida]

slip; skid

To slip over to one side or fall on a slippery surface.

past : 미끄러지 + 었어요 → 미끄러졌어요
present : 미끄러지 + 어요 → 미끄러져요
future : 미끄러지 + ㄹ 거예요 → 미끄러질 거예요

(50) 밀다 [milda]

push

To apply force against an object from one direction to move it to the opposite direction.

past : 밀 + 었어요 → 밀었어요
present : 밀 + 어요 → 밀어요
future : 밀 + ㄹ 거예요 → 밀 거예요

(51) 바라보다 [baraboda]

look; stare; gaze

To look straight at something.

past : 바라보 + 았어요 → 바라봤어요
present : 바라보 + 아요 → 바라봐요
future : 바라보 + ㄹ 거예요 → 바라볼 거예요

(52) 보다 [boda]

see; look at; notice

To perceive with eyes the existence or appearance of an object.

past : 보 + 았어요 → 봤어요
present : 보 + 아요 → 봐요
future : 보 + ㄹ 거예요 → 볼 거예요

(53) 서다 [seoda]

stand

For a human or animal to place his/her feet on the ground and assume an upright position.

past : 서 + 었어요 → 섰어요
present : 서 + 어요 → 서요
future : 서 + ㄹ 거예요 → 설 거예요

(54) 쉬다 [swida]

rest; repose; take a rest

To relax oneself to relieve one's fatigue.

past : 쉬 + 었어요 → 쉬었어요
present : 쉬 + 어요 → 쉬어요
future : 쉬 + ㄹ 거예요 → 쉴 거예요

(55) 안다 [anda]

embrace; hug; hold someone in one's arms

To open one's arms and pull someone or something toward one's bosom or make him/her or it be in one's bosom.

past : 안 + 았어요 → 안았어요
present : 안 + 아요 → 안아요
future : 안 + 을 거예요 → 안을 거예요

(56) 앉다 [anda]

sit; be seated

To place one's weight on the bottocks and put his/her body on an object or on the floor with his/her upper body in an upright position.

past : 앉 + 았어요 → 앉았어요
present : 앉 + 아요 → 앉아요
future : 앉 + 을 거예요 → 앉을 거예요

(57) 오다 [oda]

come

For something to move from another place to here.

past : 오 + 았어요 → 왔어요
present : 오 + 아요 → 와요
future : 오 + ㄹ 거예요 → 올 거예요

(58) 올라가다 [ollagada]

go up; rise; ascend

To move from the bottom to the top, or from a lower place to a higher one.

past : 올라가 + 았어요 → 올라갔어요
present : 올라가 + 아요 → 올라가요
future : 올라가 + ㄹ 거예요 → 올라갈 거예요

(59) 올라오다 [ollaoda]

come up; rise; ascend

To move from a lower place to a higher one.

past : 올라오 + 았어요 → 올라왔어요
present : 올라오 + 아요 → 올라와요
future : 올라오 + ㄹ 거예요 → 올라올 거예요

(60) 울다 [ulda]

cry

To shed tears out of unbearable joy, pain, or delight, or to make sounds while shedding tears.

past : 울 + 었어요 → 울었어요
present : 울 + 어요 → 울어요
future : 울 + ㄹ 거예요 → 울 거예요

(61) 움직이다 [umjigida]

move; budge; be in motion

For a position or posture to change; to change a position or posture.

past : 움직이 + 었어요 → 움직였어요
present : 움직이 + 어요 → 움직여요
future : 움직이 + ㄹ 거예요 → 움직일 거예요

(62) 웃다 [utda]

smile

To smile big or make a sound when one is happy or satisfied.

past : 웃 + 었어요 → 웃었어요
present : 웃 + 어요 → 웃어요
future : 웃 + 을 거예요 → 웃을 거예요

(63) 일어나다 [ireonada]

stand up; rise; sit up

To sit after lying down or stand after sitting.

past : 일어나 + 았어요 → 일어났어요
present : 일어나 + 아요 → 일어나요
future : 일어나 + ㄹ 거예요 → 일어날 거예요

(64) 일어서다 [ireoseoda]

stand up; rise to one's feet; get to one's feet

To get up from one's seat.

past : 일어서 + 었어요 → 일어섰어요
present : 일어서 + 어요 → 일어서요
future : 일어서 + ㄹ 거예요 → 일어설 거예요

(65) 잡다 [japda]

hold; grab; seize

To hold something in one's hand and not let it go.

past : 잡 + 았어요 → 잡았어요
present : 잡 + 아요 → 잡아요
future : 잡 + 을 거예요 → 잡을 거예요

(66) 접다 [jeopda]

fold

To bend a piece of cloth, paper, etc., so that one part covers another.

past : 접 + 었어요 → 접었어요
present : 접 + 어요 → 접어요
future : 접 + 을 거예요 → 접을 거예요

(67) 지나가다 [jinagada]

pass; cross

To go through a place.

past : 지나가 + 았어요 → 지나갔어요
present : 지나가 + 아요 → 지나가요
future : 지나가 + ㄹ 거예요 → 지나갈 거예요

(68) 지르다 [jireuda]

yell; shout

To shout loudly.

past : 지르 + 었어요 → 질렀어요
present : 지르 + 어요 → 질러요
future : 지르 + ㄹ 거예요 → 지를 거예요

(69) 차다 [chada]

kick

To kick or raise something powerfully with one's foot.

past : 차 + 았어요 → 찼어요
present : 차 + 아요 → 차요
future : 차 + ㄹ 거예요 → 찰 거예요

(70) 쳐다보다 [cheodaboda]

look up

To look upwards from below.

past : 쳐다보 + 았어요 → 쳐다봤어요
present : 쳐다보 + 아요 → 쳐다봐요
future : 쳐다보 + ㄹ 거예요 → 쳐다볼 거예요

(71) 치다 [chida]

hit; strike

To cause the hand or an object to bump hard against something.

past : 치 + 었어요 → 쳤어요
present : 치 + 어요 → 쳐요
future : 치 + ㄹ 거예요 → 칠 거예요

(72) 흔들다 [heundeulda]

wave; sway; flap; wag; shake

To make something move from side to side and back and forth, repeatedly.

past : 흔들 + 었어요 → 흔들었어요
present : 흔들 + 어요 → 흔들어요
future : 흔들 + ㄹ 거예요 → 흔들 거예요

(73) 기억나다 [gieongnada]

remember; recall

To recall past figures, facts, knowledge or experiences in one's mind or thought.

past : 기억나 + 았어요 → **기억났어요**
present : 기억나 + 아요 → **기억나요**
future : 기억나 + ㄹ 거예요 → **기억날 거예요**

(74) 모르다 [moreuda]

not know

To have no knowledge or understanding of a person, object or fact.

past : 모르 + 았어요 → **몰랐어요**
present : 모르 + 아요 → **몰라요**
future : 모르 + ㄹ 거예요 → **모를 거예요**

(75) 믿다 [mitda]

believe; trust

To think of something as being right or true.

past : 믿 + 었어요 → **믿었어요**
present : 믿 + 어요 → **믿어요**
future : 믿 + 을 거예요 → **믿을 거예요**

(76) 바라다 [barada]

want; hope; wish

To expect that something could be done as one's thought or hope.

past : 바라 + 았어요 → **바랐어요**
present : 바라 + 아요 → **바라요**
future : 바라 + ㄹ 거예요 → **바랄 거예요**

(77) 보이다 [boida]

show; reveal

To make someone know the presence or outward appearance of an object by looking at it.

past : 보이 + 었어요 → 보였어요
present : 보이 + 어요 → 보여요
future : 보이 + ㄹ 거예요 → 보일 거예요

(78) 생각나다 [saenggangnada]

occur

For a new idea to come to one's head.

past : 생각나 + 았어요 → 생각났어요
present : 생각나 + 아요 → 생각나요
future : 생각나 + ㄹ 거예요 → 생각날 거예요

(79) 알다 [alda]

know; understand

To have information or knowledge about an object or situation through education, experience, thoughts, etc.

past : 알 + 았어요 → 알았어요
present : 알 + 아요 → 알아요
future : 알 + ㄹ 거예요 → 알 거예요

(80) 알리다 [allida]

inform; tell; notify

To let someone realize or know what he/she did not know or forgot.

past : 알리 + 었어요 → 알렸어요
present : 알리 + 어요 → 알려요
future : 알리 + ㄹ 거예요 → 알릴 거예요

(81) 외우다 [oeuda]

memorize

To not forget but to remember a speech, composition, etc.

past : 외우 + 었어요 → **외웠어요**
present : 외우 + 어요 → **외워요**
future : 외우 + ㄹ 거예요 → **외울 거예요**

(82) 원하다 [wonhada]

want; wish; hope

To hope for something or desire to do something.

past : 원하 + 였어요 → **원했어요**
present : 원하 + 여요 → **원해요**
future : 원하 + ㄹ 거예요 → **원할 거예요**

(83) 잊다 [itda]

forget; be forgetful of

To not remember or fail to remember something that one knew once.

past : 잊 + 었어요 → **잊었어요**
present : 잊 + 어요 → **잊어요**
future : 잊 + 을 거예요 → **잊을 거예요**

(84) 잊어버리다 [ijeobeorida]

forget; be forgetful of

To not remember or fail to remember something that one knew once.

past : 잊어버리 + 었어요 → **잊어버렸어요**
present : 잊어버리 + 어요 → **잊어버려요**
future : 잊어버리 + ㄹ 거예요 → **잊어버릴 거예요**

(85) 기르다 [gireuda]

breed; grow; cultivate

To give food or nutrients and protect animals and plants to make them grow.

past : 기르 + 었어요 → 길렀어요
present : 기르 + 어요 → 길러요
future : 기르 + ㄹ 거예요 → 기를 거예요

(86) 살다 [salda]

live; be alive

To be alive.

past : 살 + 았어요 → 살았어요
present : 살 + 아요 → 살아요
future : 살 + ㄹ 거예요 → 살 거예요

(87) 죽다 [jukda]

die

For a living plant, animal, or insect to lose its life.

past : 죽 + 었어요 → 죽었어요
present : 죽 + 어요 → 죽어요
future : 죽 + 을 거예요 → 죽을 거예요

(88) 지내다 [jinaeda]

live

To live in a certain state or condition.

past : 지내 + 었어요 → 지냈어요
present : 지내 + 어요 → 지내요
future : 지내 + ㄹ 거예요 → 지낼 거예요

(89) 태어나다 [taeeonada]

be born

For a person, animal, etc., to take form and come out of the mother's body.

past : 태어나 + 았어요 → 태어났어요
present : 태어나 + 아요 → 태어나요
future : 태어나 + ㄹ 거예요 → 태어날 거예요

(90) 감다 [gamda]

close; shut eyes

To cover one's eyes with one's eyelids.

past : 감 + 았어요 → 감았어요
present : 감 + 아요 → 감아요
future : 감 + 을 거예요 → 감을 거예요

(91) 깨다 [kkaeda]

wake up

To wake up from a sleeping state and come to one's senses; to do something in such a way.

past : 깨 + 었어요 → 깼어요
present : 깨 + 어요 → 깨요
future : 깨 + ㄹ 거예요 → 깰 거예요

(92) 꾸다 [kkuda]

dream

To see, hear, and feel in a dream as if it were real.

past : 꾸 + 었어요 → 꾸었어요
present : 꾸 + 어요 → 꾸어요
future : 꾸 + ㄹ 거예요 → 꿀 거예요

(93) 눕다 [nupda]

lie down; lay oneself down; lie

For a person or animal to lie with the back or flank horizontally to touch a certain place.

past : 눕 + 었어요 → 누웠어요
present : 눕 + 어요 → 누워요
future : 눕 + ㄹ 거예요 → 누울 거예요

(94) 다녀오다 [danyeooda]

go and come back

To go to a certain place and then return from it.

past : 다녀오 + 았어요 → 다녀왔어요
present : 다녀오 + 아요 → 다녀와요
future : 다녀오 + ㄹ 거예요 → 다녀올 거예요

(95) 다니다 [danida]

go continuously

To constantly go to a place.

past : 다니 + 었어요 → 다녔어요
present : 다니 + 어요 → 다녀요
future : 다니 + ㄹ 거예요 → 다닐 거예요

(96) 닦다 [dakda]

wipe; scrub

To rub to eliminate dirty things.

past : 닦 + 았어요 → 닦았어요
present : 닦 + 아요 → 닦아요
future : 닦 + 을 거예요 → 닦을 거예요

(97) 씻다 [ssitda]

wash

To clean something by removing dirt or grime.

past : 씻 + 었어요 → 씻었어요
present : 씻 + 어요 → 씻어요
future : 씻 + 을 거예요 → 씻을 거예요

(98) 일어나다 [ireonada]

get up

To wake up.

past : 일어나 + 았어요 → 일어났어요
present : 일어나 + 아요 → 일어나요
future : 일어나 + ㄹ 거예요 → 일어날 거예요

(99) 자다 [jada]

sleep

To be in the state of taking a rest for a period of time with one's eyes closed and mental activities suspended.

past : 자 + 았어요 → 잤어요
present : 자 + 아요 → 자요
future : 자 + ㄹ 거예요 → 잘 거예요

(100) 잠자다 [jamjada]

sleep; have a sleep

To stop the activities of one's body and mind and rest for a while.

past : 잠자 + 았어요 → 잠잤어요
present : 잠자 + 아요 → 잠자요
future : 잠자 + ㄹ 거예요 → 잠잘 거예요

(101) 주무시다 [jumusida]

sleep

(honorific) To sleep.

past : 주무시 + 었어요 → 주무셨어요
present : 주무시 + 어요 → 주무셔요
future : 주무시 + ㄹ 거예요 → 주무실 거예요

(102) 구경하다 [gugyeonghada]

watch

To see something with interest.

past : 구경하 + 였어요 → 구경했어요
present : 구경하 + 여요 → 구경해요
future : 구경하 + ㄹ 거예요 → 구경할 거예요

(103) 그리다 [geurida]

draw; paint

To express an object in lines or colors by using a pencil, brush, etc.

past : 그리 + 었어요 → 그렸어요
present : 그리 + 어요 → 그려요
future : 그리 + ㄹ 거예요 → 그릴 거예요

(104) 노래하다 [noraehada]

sing

To sing a piece of composition created by setting rhythmical lyrics to music.

past : 노래하 + 였어요 → 노래했어요
present : 노래하 + 여요 → 노래해요
future : 노래하 + ㄹ 거예요 → 노래할 거예요

(105) 놀다 [nolda]

play; have fun

To have a good time while playing.

past : 놀 + 았어요 → 놀았어요
present : 놀 + 아요 → 놀아요
future : 놀 + ㄹ 거예요 → 놀 거예요

(106) 독서하다 [dokseohada]

read

To read a book.

past : 독서하 + 였어요 → 독서했어요
present : 독서하 + 여요 → 독서해요
future : 독서하 + ㄹ 거예요 → 독서할 거예요

(107) 등산하다 [deungsanhada]

hike; climb

To climb a mountain with the purpose of exercising, amusement, etc.

past : 등산하 + 였어요 → 등산했어요
present : 등산하 + 여요 → 등산해요
future : 등산하 + ㄹ 거예요 → 등산할 거예요

(108) 부르다 [bureuda]

sing

To sing to a tune.

past : 부르 + 었어요 → 불렀어요
present : 부르 + 어요 → 불러요
future : 부르 + ㄹ 거예요 → 부를 거예요

(109) 불다 [bulda]

blow; play

To put a wind instrument to the mouth and exhale to make a sound.

past : 불 + 었어요 → 불었어요
present : 불 + 어요 → 불어요
future : 불 + ㄹ 거예요 → 불 거예요

(110) 산책하다 [sanchaekada]

walk; stroll

To walk slowly around a nearby place for rest or health.

past : 산책하 + 였어요 → 산책했어요
present : 산책하 + 여요 → 산책해요
future : 산책하 + ㄹ 거예요 → 산책할 거예요

(111) 수영하다 [suyeonghada]

swim

To swim in the water.

past : 수영하 + 였어요 → 수영했어요
present : 수영하 + 여요 → 수영해요
future : 수영하 + ㄹ 거예요 → 수영할 거예요

(112) 여행하다 [yeohaenghada]

travel; trip

To go away from home, and visit other places or foreign countries and do sightseeing.

past : 여행하 + 였어요 → 여행했어요
present : 여행하 + 여요 → 여행해요
future : 여행하 + ㄹ 거예요 → 여행할 거예요

(113) 운동하다 [undonghada]

exercise; take exercise

To move one's body in order to train it or improve one's health.

past : 운동하 + 였어요 → 운동했어요
present : 운동하 + 여요 → 운동해요
future : 운동하 + ㄹ 거예요 → 운동할 거예요

(114) 즐기다 [jeulgida]

appreciate; enjoy; delight in

To enjoy to the fullest.

past : 즐기 + 었어요 → 즐겼어요
present : 즐기 + 어요 → 즐겨요
future : 즐기 + ㄹ 거예요 → 즐길 거예요

(115) 찍다 [jjikda]

take

To transfer an image of an object to a film through a camera.

past : 찍 + 었어요 → 찍었어요
present : 찍 + 어요 → 찍어요
future : 찍 + 을 거예요 → 찍을 거예요

(116) 추다 [chuda]

dance

To perform the movements of a dance.

past : 추 + 었어요 → 췄어요
present : 추 + 어요 → 춰요
future : 추 + ㄹ 거예요 → 출 거예요

(117) 춤추다 [chumchuda]

dance

To move one's body to a piece of music or a regular beat.

past : 춤추 + 었어요 → 춤췄어요
present : 춤추 + 어요 → 춤춰요
future : 춤추 + ㄹ 거예요 → 춤출 거예요

(118) 켜다 [kyeoda]

play

To make a sound by rubbing the strings of a string instrument with a bow.

past : 켜 + 었어요 → 켰어요
present : 켜 + 어요 → 켜요
future : 켜 + ㄹ 거예요 → 켤 거예요

(119) 타다 [tada]

ride

To sit or stand on such play equipment as a swing, seesaw, etc., and to move back and forth or up and down.

quá khứ : 타 + 았어요 → 탔어요
hiện tại : 타 + 아요 → 타요
tương lai : 타 + ㄹ 거예요 → 탈 거예요

(120) 검사하다 [geomsahada]

examine; inspect

To investigate or examine a certain incident or object to decide whether it is right or wrong, or good or bad.

past : 검사하 + 였어요 → 검사했어요
present : 검사하 + 여요 → 검사해요
future : 검사하 + ㄹ 거예요 → 검사할 거예요

(121) 고치다 [gochida]

heal

To cure a disease.

past : 고치 + 었어요 → **고쳤어요**
present : 고치 + 어요 → **고쳐요**
future : 고치 + ㄹ 거예요 → **고칠 거예요**

(122) 바르다 [bareuda]

apply; spread; put on

To put liquid, powder, etc., on the surface of an object and spread it evenly.

past : 바르 + 았어요 → **발랐어요**
present : 바르 + 아요 → **발라요**
future : 바르 + ㄹ 거예요 → **바를 거예요**

(123) 수술하다 [susulhada]

operate

To slit, cut, attach, and stitch a body part or organ in order to treat an illness.

past : 수술하 + 였어요 → **수술했어요**
present : 수술하 + 여요 → **수술해요**
future : 수술하 + ㄹ 거예요 → **수술할 거예요**

(124) 입원하다 [ibwonhada]

be hospitalized

To stay in a hospital for a certain period of time to have one's disease treated.

past : 입원하 + 였어요 → **입원했어요**
present : 입원하 + 여요 → **입원해요**
future : 입원하 + ㄹ 거예요 → **입원할 거예요**

(125) 퇴원하다 [toewonhada]

leave the hospital; be discharged from the hospital

To leave the hospital after one stayed there for a certain period of time to have one's disease treated.

past : 퇴원하 + 였어요 → 퇴원했어요
present : 퇴원하 + 여요 → 퇴원해요
future : 퇴원하 + ㄹ 거예요 → 퇴원할 거예요

(126) 먹다 [meokda]

eat; have; consume; take

To put food into one's mouth and take it in one's stomach.

past : 먹 + 었어요 → 먹었어요
present : 먹 + 어요 → 먹어요
future : 먹 + 을 거예요 → 먹을 거예요

(127) 마시다 [masida]

drink

To make liquid such as water, etc., pass down one's throat.

past : 마시 + 었어요 → 마셨어요
present : 마시 + 어요 → 마셔요
future : 마시 + ㄹ 거예요 → 마실 거예요

(128) 굽다 [gupda]

bake; roast; grill

To cook food over a fire.

past : 굽 + 었어요 → 구웠어요
present : 굽 + 어요 → 구워요
future : 굽 + ㄹ 거예요 → 구울 거예요

(129) 깎다 [kkakda]

peel

To remove the surface of something or the skin of a fruit, etc., with a tool such as a knife.

past : 깎 + 았어요 → 깎았어요
present : 깎 + 아요 → 깎아요
future : 깎 + 을 거예요 → 깎을 거예요

(130) 끓다 [kkeulta]

boil

For liquid to become very hot and bubble.

past : 끓 + 었어요 → 끓었어요
present : 끓 + 어요 → 끓어요
future : 끓 + 을 거예요 → 끓을 거예요

(131) 끓이다 [kkeurida]

boil

To heat up liquid to such a high temperature that it bubbles and boils.

past : 끓이 + 었어요 → 끓였어요
present : 끓이 + 어요 → 끓여요
future : 끓이 + ㄹ 거예요 → 끓일 거예요

(132) 볶다 [bokda]

stir-fry

To drain most of water from ingredients, put them in a frying pan, and cook them over heat while stirring continuously.

past : 볶 + 았어요 → 볶았어요
present : 볶 + 아요 → 볶아요
future : 볶 + 을 거예요 → 볶을 거예요

(133) 섞다 [seokda]

mix

To put two or more things together in one container or place.

past : 섞 + 었어요 → 섞었어요
present : 섞 + 어요 → 섞어요
future : 섞 + 을 거예요 → 섞을 거예요

(134) 썰다 [sseolda]

slice; cut

To cut something into several pieces by pressing a knife, saw, etc., downwards and moving the blade forwards and backwards.

past : 썰 + 었어요 → 썰었어요
present : 썰 + 어요 → 썰어요
future : 썰 + ㄹ 거예요 → 썰 거예요

(135) 씹다 [ssipda]

chew; masticate

For a person or animal to cut food into small bits or grind it into a soft state with the teeth.

past : 씹 + 었어요 → 씹었어요
present : 씹 + 어요 → 씹어요
future : 씹 + 을 거예요 → 씹을 거예요

(136) 익다 [ikda]

be cooked

For raw meat, vegetables, grains, etc., to be changed in taste and characteristics after being heated.

past : 익 + 었어요 → 익었어요
present : 익 + 어요 → 익어요
future : 익 + 을 거예요 → 익을 거예요

(137) 찌다 [jjida]

steam

To cook or heat up food with hot steam.

past : 찌 + 었어요 → 쪘어요
present : 찌 + 어요 → 쪄요
future : 찌 + ㄹ 거예요 → 찔 거예요

(138) 타다 [tada]

be overcooked

For food to be overcooked until it becomes blackish.

past : 타 + 았어요 → 탔어요
present : 타 + 아요 → 타요
future : 타 + ㄹ 거예요 → 탈 거예요

(139) 튀기다 [twigida]

fry

To put an ingredient in boiling oil, so that it inflates.

past : 튀기 + 었어요 → 튀겼어요
present : 튀기 + 어요 → 튀겨요
future : 튀기 + ㄹ 거예요 → 튀길 거예요

(140) 갈아입다 [garaipda]

change one's clothes

To take off one's clothes and put on other clothes.

past : 갈아입 + 었어요 → 갈아입었어요
present : 갈아입 + 어요 → 갈아입어요
future : 갈아입 + 을 거예요 → 갈아입을 거예요

(141) 끼다 [kkida]

stick in; fasten

To put something inside a gap and tighten it to prevent it from falling out.

past : 끼 + 었어요 → 꼈어요
present : 끼 + 어요 → 껴요
future : 끼 + ㄹ 거예요 → 낄 거예요

(142) 매다 [maeda]

tie; bind; lace

To tie two ends of a cord or rope not to fall apart.

past : 매 + 었어요 → 맸어요
present : 매 + 어요 → 매요
future : 매 + ㄹ 거예요 → 맬 거예요

(143) 벗다 [beotda]

take off

To have an object, clothes, etc., taken off one's body.

past : 벗 + 었어요 → 벗었어요
present : 벗 + 어요 → 벗어요
future : 벗 + 을 거예요 → 벗을 거예요

(144) 신다 [sinda]

put on; wear

To put one's feet into a pair of shoes, socks, etc., and cover the whole or a part of the feet with them.

past : 신 + 었어요 → 신었어요
present : 신 + 어요 → 신어요
future : 신 + 을 거예요 → 신을 거예요

(145) 쓰다 [sseuda]

wear; put on

To cover one's head with a hat, wig, etc.

past : 쓰 + 었어요 → 썼어요
present : 쓰 + 어요 → 써요
future : 쓰 + ㄹ 거예요 → 쓸 거예요

(146) 입다 [ipda]

wear; be dressed; put on

To hang or drape clothes on or around one's body.

past : 입 + 었어요 → 입었어요
present : 입 + 어요 → 입어요
future : 입 + 을 거예요 → 입을 거예요

(147) 차다 [chada]

wear

To attach, hang, or put an object on one's waist, wrist, ankle, etc.

past : 차 + 았어요 → 찼어요
present : 차 + 아요 → 차요
future : 차 + ㄹ 거예요 → 찰 거예요

(148) 기르다 [gireuda]

grow

To make one's hair, mustache, etc., grow long.

past : 기르 + 었어요 → 길렀어요
present : 기르 + 어요 → 길러요
future : 기르 + ㄹ 거예요 → 기를 거예요

(149) 깎다 [kkakda]

cut

To make grass, hair, etc. short by cutting it.

past : 깎 + 았어요 → 깎았어요
present : 깎 + 아요 → 깎아요
future : 깎 + 을 거예요 → 깎을 거예요

(150) 드라이하다 [deuraihada]

dry

To dry or style hair by using an electric device that blows air.

past : 드라이하 + 였어요 → 드라이했어요
present : 드라이하 + 여요 → 드라이해요
future : 드라이하 + ㄹ 거예요 → 드라이할 거예요

(151) 면도하다 [myeondohada]

shave

To cut off the beard or hair on one's face or body.

past : 면도하 + 였어요 → 면도했어요
present : 면도하 + 여요 → 면도해요
future : 면도하 + ㄹ 거예요 → 면도할 거예요

(152) 빗다 [bitda]

comb

To arrange hair, fur, etc., with a comb, hand, etc.

past : 빗 + 었어요 → 빗었어요
present : 빗 + 어요 → 빗어요
future : 빗 + 을 거예요 → 빗을 거예요

(153) 염색하다 [yeomsaekada]

dye

To color cloth, thread, hair, etc.

past : 염색하 + 였어요 → **염색했어요**
present : 염색하 + 여요 → **염색해요**
future : 염색하 + ㄹ 거예요 → **염색할 거예요**

(154) 이발하다 [ibalhada]

have one's hair cut; have haircut

To have one's hair cut and groomed.

past : 이발하 + 였어요 → **이발했어요**
present : 이발하 + 여요 → **이발해요**
future : 이발하 + ㄹ 거예요 → **이발할 거예요**

(155) 파마하다 [pamahada]

get a perm; have one's hair permed

To have one's hair curled or straightened, so that it stays that way for a long time, using a machine or chemical substance.

past : 파마하 + 였어요 → **파마했어요**
present : 파마하 + 여요 → **파마해요**
future : 파마하 + ㄹ 거예요 → **파마할 거예요**

(156) 화장하다 [hwajanghada]

put on make-up; adorn oneself

To make oneself up by applying cosmetics over the face.

past : 화장하 + 였어요 → **화장했어요**
present : 화장하 + 여요 → **화장해요**
future : 화장하 + ㄹ 거예요 → **화장할 거예요**

(157) 이사하다 [isahada]

move; change one's abode

To leave the place where one has lived, and move into another place.

past : 이사하 + 였어요 → 이사했어요
present : 이사하 + 여요 → 이사해요
future : 이사하 + ㄹ 거예요 → 이사할 거예요

(158) 머무르다 [meomureuda]

stay temporarily; stop over; anchor

To stop in one's way or to stay at a place temporarily.

past : 머무르 + 었어요 → 머물렀어요
present : 머무르 + 어요 → 머물러요
future : 머무르 + ㄹ 거예요 → 머무를 거예요

(159) 묵다 [mukda]

stay; lodge

To stay in a place as a guest.

past : 묵 + 었어요 → 묵었어요
present : 묵 + 어요 → 묵어요
future : 묵 + 을 거예요 → 묵을 거예요

(160) 숙박하다 [sukbakada]

stay; be accommodated; lodge

To sleep and stay at an inn, hotel, etc.

past : 숙박하 + 였어요 → 숙박했어요
present : 숙박하 + 여요 → 숙박해요
future : 숙박하 + ㄹ 거예요 → 숙박할 거예요

(161) 체류하다 [cheryuhada]

stay; sojourn

To be away from home and stay at a place.

past : 체류하 + 였어요 → 체류했어요
present : 체류하 + 여요 → 체류해요
future : 체류하 + ㄹ 거예요 → 체류할 거예요

(162) 걸다 [geolda]

hang

To hang a certain object somewhere so as to prevent it from falling.

past : 걸 + 었어요 → 걸었어요
present : 걸 + 어요 → 걸어요
future : 걸 + ㄹ 거예요 → 걸 거예요

(163) 고치다 [gochida]

repair; mend

To fix something broken so that it can be used again.

past : 고치 + 었어요 → 고쳤어요
present : 고치 + 어요 → 고쳐요
future : 고치 + ㄹ 거예요 → 고칠 거예요

(164) 끄다 [kkeuda]

put out; extinguish

To stop a fire from burning.

past : 끄 + 었어요 → 껐어요
present : 끄 + 어요 → 꺼요
future : 끄 + ㄹ 거예요 → 끌 거예요

(165) 빨다 [ppalda]

wash; clean

To put clothes, etc., in water and rub them with one's hands, or remove dirt on them by using a washing machine.

past : 빨 + 았어요 → 빨았어요
present : 빨 + 아요 → 빨아요
future : 빨 + ㄹ 거예요 → 빨 거예요

(166) 설거지하다 [seolgeojihada]

wash the dishes; do the dishes

To wash and put away the dishes after eating.

past : 설거지하 + 였어요 → 설거지했어요
present : 설거지하 + 여요 → 설거지해요
future : 설거지하 + ㄹ 거예요 → 설거지할 거예요

(167) 세탁하다 [setakada]

wash; do the laundry

To wash dirty clothes, etc.

past : 세탁하 + 였어요 → 세탁했어요
present : 세탁하 + 여요 → 세탁해요
future : 세탁하 + ㄹ 거예요 → 세탁할 거예요

(168) 정리하다 [jeongnihada]

organize

To gather or clear away dispersed or unorganized items.

past : 정리하 + 였어요 → 정리했어요
present : 정리하 + 여요 → 정리해요
future : 정리하 + ㄹ 거예요 → 정리할 거예요

(169) 청소하다 [cheongsohada]

clean

To clean something dirty and messy.

past : 청소하 + 였어요 → 청소했어요
present : 청소하 + 여요 → 청소해요
future : 청소하 + ㄹ 거예요 → 청소할 거예요

(170) 켜다 [kyeoda]

light; ignite; set

To light an oil lamp or candle, or to set a flame using a matchstick or lighter.

past : 켜 + 었어요 → 켰어요
present : 켜 + 어요 → 켜요
future : 켜 + ㄹ 거예요 → 켤 거예요

(171) 말리다 [mallida]

dry; make dry; air

To make moisture evaporate and disappear.

past : 말리 + 었어요 → 말렸어요
present : 말리 + 어요 → 말려요
future : 말리 + ㄹ 거예요 → 말릴 거예요

(172) 삶다 [samda]

boil

To put in water and boil.

past : 삶 + 았어요 → 삶았어요
present : 삶 + 아요 → 삶아요
future : 삶 + 을 거예요 → 삶을 거예요

(173) 쓸다 [sseulda]

sweep

To gather things together and then clear them off a certain place.

past : 쓸 + 었어요 → 쓸었어요
present : 쓸 + 어요 → 쓸어요
future : 쓸 + ㄹ 거예요 → 쓸 거예요

(174) 가져가다 [gajeogada]

bring

To move an object from one place to another place.

past : 가져가 + 았어요 → 가져갔어요
present : 가져가 + 아요 → 가져가요
future : 가져가 + ㄹ 거예요 → 가져갈 거예요

(175) 가져오다 [gajeooda]

bring

To bring an object from one place to another place.

past : 가져오 + 았어요 → 가져왔어요
present : 가져오 + 아요 → 가져와요
future : 가져오 + ㄹ 거예요 → 가져올 거예요

(176) 거절하다 [geojeolhada]

refuse; reject; deny

Not to accept a request, proposal or gift from another person.

past : 거절하 + 였어요 → 거절했어요
present : 거절하 + 여요 → 거절해요
future : 거절하 + ㄹ 거예요 → 거절할 거예요

(177) 걸다 [geolda]

call

To make a call.

past : 걸 + 었어요 → 걸었어요
present : 걸 + 어요 → 걸어요
future : 걸 + ㄹ 거예요 → 걸 거예요

(178) 기다리다 [gidarida]

wait

To spend time until a person or time comes or a certain event is realized.

past : 기다리 + 었어요 → 기다렸어요
present : 기다리 + 어요 → 기다려요
future : 기다리 + ㄹ 거예요 → 기다릴 거예요

(179) 나누다 [nanuda]

divide; split

To divide something that was one into two or more parts or pieces.

past : 나누 + 었어요 → 나눴어요
present : 나누 + 어요 → 나눠요
future : 나누 + ㄹ 거예요 → 나눌 거예요

(180) 데려가다 [deryeogada]

take someone away; take someone with one

To make someone follow one, and thus go with him/her.

past : 데려가 + 았어요 → 데려갔어요
present : 데려가 + 아요 → 데려가요
future : 데려가 + ㄹ 거예요 → 데려갈 거예요

(181) 데려오다 [deryeooda]

bring someone with one; come in company with

To make someone follow one, and thus come with him/her.

past : 데려오 + 았어요 → 데려왔어요
present : 데려오 + 아요 → 데려와요
future : 데려오 + ㄹ 거예요 → 데려올 거예요

(182) 데이트하다 [deiteuhada]

date; go out with

For a man and a woman to meet to go out.

past : 데이트하 + 였어요 → 데이트했어요
present : 데이트하 + 여요 → 데이트해요
future : 데이트하 + ㄹ 거예요 → 데이트할 거예요

(183) 도와주다 [dowajuda]

help; assist

To help someone with something, or give support.

past : 도와주 + 었어요 → 도와줬어요
present : 도와주 + 어요 → 도와줘요
future : 도와주 + ㄹ 거예요 → 도와줄 거예요

(184) 돌려주다 [dollyeojuda]

give back; return

To give back or pay back something borrowed, taken, or received from the owner.

past : 돌려주 + 었어요 → 돌려줬어요
present : 돌려주 + 어요 → 돌려줘요
future : 돌려주 + ㄹ 거예요 → 돌려줄 거예요

(185) 돕다 [dopda]

help; assist

To help someone with his/her work or do something that supports him/her.

past : 돕 + 았어요 → 도왔어요
present : 돕 + 아요 → 도와요
future : 돕 + ㄹ 거예요 → 도울 거예요

(186) 드리다 [deurida]

give; offer

(honorific) To give; to hand something over to someone or allow someone to use it.

past : 드리 + 었어요 → 드렸어요
present : 드리 + 어요 → 드려요
future : 드리 + ㄹ 거예요 → 드릴 거예요

(187) 만나다 [mannada]

meet; meet with; join

For one of two to go or come and be face to face with the other.

past : 만나 + 았어요 → 만났어요
present : 만나 + 아요 → 만나요
future : 만나 + ㄹ 거예요 → 만날 거예요

(188) 바꾸다 [bakkuda]

change; exchange; replace; turn into

To remove something and replace it with another.

past : 바꾸 + 었어요 → 바꿨어요
present : 바꾸 + 어요 → 바꿔요
future : 바꾸 + ㄹ 거예요 → 바꿀 거예요

(189) 받다 [batda]

receive; get

To take something that someone else has given or sent.

past : 받 + 았어요 → **받았어요**
present : 받 + 아요 → **받아요**
future : 받 + 을 거예요 → **받을 거예요**

(190) 방문하다 [bangmunhada]

visit

To go to a certain place in order to meet a person or see something.

past : 방문하 + 였어요 → **방문했어요**
present : 방문하 + 여요 → **방문해요**
future : 방문하 + ㄹ 거예요 → **방문할 거예요**

(191) 보내다 [bonaeda]

send

To make a person, goods, etc., go somewhere else.

past : 보내 + 었어요 → **보냈어요**
present : 보내 + 어요 → **보내요**
future : 보내 + ㄹ 거예요 → **보낼 거예요**

(192) 보다 [boda]

watch; see; enjoy

To enjoy or appreciate an object with eyes.

past : 보 + 았어요 → **봤어요**
present : 보 + 아요 → **봐요**
future : 보 + ㄹ 거예요 → **볼 거예요**

(193) 뵈다 [boeda]

meet; see

To meet someone older or with a higher position than oneself.

past : 뵈 + 었어요 → 뵀어요
present : 뵈 + 어요 → 봬요
future : 뵈 + ㄹ 거예요 → 뵐 거예요

(194) 부탁하다 [butakada]

request

To ask someone to do something or entrust someone with something.

past : 부탁하 + 였어요 → 부탁했어요
present : 부탁하 + 여요 → 부탁해요
future : 부탁하 + ㄹ 거예요 → 부탁할 거예요

(195) 사귀다 [sagwida]

get along with; go around with; go out with

To come to know and keep each other's company.

past : 사귀 + 었어요 → 사귀었어요
present : 사귀 + 어요 → 사귀어요
future : 사귀 + ㄹ 거예요 → 사귈 거예요

(196) 세배하다 [sebaehada]

perform new year's bow

To perform a traditional bow to pay respect to one's elders on New Year's Day.

past : 세배하 + 였어요 → 세배했어요
present : 세배하 + 여요 → 세배해요
future : 세배하 + ㄹ 거예요 → 세배할 거예요

(197) 소개하다 [sogaehada]

introduce

To help people to get to know each other or start a relationship.

past : 소개하 + 였어요 → 소개했어요
present : 소개하 + 여요 → 소개해요
future : 소개하 + ㄹ 거예요 → 소개할 거예요

(198) 신청하다 [sincheonghada]

apply

To make an official request to an organization, institution, etc., asking for it to do something.

past : 신청하 + 였어요 → 신청했어요
present : 신청하 + 여요 → 신청해요
future : 신청하 + ㄹ 거예요 → 신청할 거예요

(199) 실례하다 [sillyehada]

commit a breach of etiquette; commit a discourtesy

For one's remark or behavior to be impolite.

past : 실례하 + 였어요 → 실례했어요
present : 실례하 + 여요 → 실례해요
future : 실례하 + ㄹ 거예요 → 실례할 거예요

(200) 싸우다 [ssauda]

fight; quarrel; dispute

To try to win by argument or force.

past : 싸우 + 었어요 → 싸웠어요
present : 싸우 + 어요 → 싸워요
future : 싸우 + ㄹ 거예요 → 싸울 거예요

(201) 안내하다 [annaehada]

make known

To introduce something to someone, helping him/her know it.

past : 안내하 + 였어요 → **안내했어요**
present : 안내하 + 여요 → **안내해요**
future : 안내하 + ㄹ 거예요 → **안내할 거예요**

(202) 약속하다 [yaksokada]

promise; pledge; make an appointment

To agree with someone to do a certain thing.

past : 약속하 + 였어요 → **약속했어요**
present : 약속하 + 여요 → **약속해요**
future : 약속하 + ㄹ 거예요 → **약속할 거예요**

(203) 얻다 [eotda]

get; receive

To take and have something without special efforts or without paying for it.

past : 얻 + 었어요 → **얻었어요**
present : 얻 + 어요 → **얻어요**
future : 얻 + 을 거예요 → **얻을 거예요**

(204) 연락하다 [yeollakada]

notify; communicate; speak to

To deliver a fact in order to inform someone of it.

past : 연락하 + 였어요 → **연락했어요**
present : 연락하 + 여요 → **연락해요**
future : 연락하 + ㄹ 거예요 → **연락할 거예요**

(205) 이기다 [igida]
win; beat; defeat
To beat and perform better than one´s opponent in a bet, match, fight, etc.

past : 이기 + 었어요 → 이겼어요
present : 이기 + 어요 → 이겨요
future : 이기 + ㄹ 거예요 → 이길 거예요

(206) 인사하다 [insahada]
greet; salute
To show courtesy when meeting or saying goodbye to someone.

past : 인사하 + 였어요 → 인사했어요
present : 인사하 + 여요 → 인사해요
future : 인사하 + ㄹ 거예요 → 인사할 거예요

(207) 전하다 [jeonhada]
give; hand; pass on
To deliver something to someone.

past : 전하 + 였어요 → 전했어요
present : 전하 + 여요 → 전해요
future : 전하 + ㄹ 거예요 → 전할 거예요

(208) 정하다 [jeonghada]
decide
To choose one among many.

past : 정하 + 였어요 → 정했어요
present : 정하 + 여요 → 정해요
future : 정하 + ㄹ 거예요 → 정할 거예요

(209) 주다 [juda]

give

To give an item to someone else so he/she can have or use it.

past : 주 + 었어요 → 줬어요
present : 주 + 어요 → 줘요
future : 주 + ㄹ 거예요 → 줄 거예요

(210) 지다 [jida]

lose

To fail to defeat one's opponent in a match, fight, etc.

past : 지 + 었어요 → 졌어요
present : 지 + 어요 → 져요
future : 지 + ㄹ 거예요 → 질 거예요

(211) 지키다 [jikida]

obey; observe

To keep a promise or comply with etiquette rules, regulations, etc.

past : 지키 + 었어요 → 지켰어요
present : 지키 + 어요 → 지켜요
future : 지키 + ㄹ 거예요 → 지킬 거예요

(212) 찾아가다 [chajagada]

go visiting

To go to a place to meet someone or do something.

past : 찾아가 + 았어요 → 찾아갔어요
present : 찾아가 + 아요 → 찾아가요
future : 찾아가 + ㄹ 거예요 → 찾아갈 거예요

(213) 찾아오다 [chajaoda]

come visiting

To go to a place to meet someone or do something.

past : 찾아오 + 았어요 → **찾아왔어요**
present : 찾아오 + 아요 → **찾아와요**
future : 찾아오 + ㄹ 거예요 → **찾아올 거예요**

(214) 초대하다 [chodaehada]

invite

To ask someone to come to a certain place, gathering, event, etc.

past : 초대하 + 였어요 → **초대했어요**
present : 초대하 + 여요 → **초대해요**
future : 초대하 + ㄹ 거예요 → **초대할 거예요**

(215) 축하하다 [chukahada]

congratulate; celebrate

To greet someone with pleasure, commenting on his/her happy occasion, achievement, etc.

past : 축하하 + 였어요 → **축하했어요**
present : 축하하 + 여요 → **축하해요**
future : 축하하 + ㄹ 거예요 → **축하할 거예요**

(216) 취소하다 [chwisohada]

cancel

To take back what has been announced, or revoke what has been promised or planned.

past : 취소하 + 였어요 → **취소했어요**
present : 취소하 + 여요 → **취소해요**
future : 취소하 + ㄹ 거예요 → **취소할 거예요**

(217) 헤어지다 [heeojida]
part; bid farewell; say good-bye
To part with another one has been with.

past : 헤어지 + 었어요 → 헤어졌어요
present : 헤어지 + 어요 → 헤어져요
future : 헤어지 + ㄹ 거예요 → 헤어질 거예요

(218) 환영하다 [hwanyeonghada]
welcome; greet
To receive someone arriving gladly and cordially.

past : 환영하 + 였어요 → 환영했어요
present : 환영하 + 여요 → 환영해요
future : 환영하 + ㄹ 거예요 → 환영할 거예요

(219) 갈아타다 [garatada]
transfer; transship
To get off from a vehicle and get on another.

past : 갈아타 + 았어요 → 갈아탔어요
present : 갈아타 + 아요 → 갈아타요
future : 갈아타 + ㄹ 거예요 → 갈아탈 거예요

(220) 건너가다 [geonneogada]
cross; go across
To move from one place to another across a river, bridge, road, etc.

past : 건너가 + 았어요 → 건너갔어요
present : 건너가 + 아요 → 건너가요
future : 건너가 + ㄹ 거예요 → 건너갈 거예요

(221) 건너다 [geonneoda]

cross; go across

To cross or pass through something to move over to the opposite side of it.

past : 건너 + 었어요 → 건넜어요
present : 건너 + 어요 → 건너요
future : 건너 + ㄹ 거예요 → 건널 거예요

(222) 내리다 [naerida]

get off; come out

To touch a certain spot, after coming outside from a vehicle.

past : 내리 + 었어요 → 내렸어요
present : 내리 + 어요 → 내려요
future : 내리 + ㄹ 거예요 → 내릴 거예요

(223) 도착하다 [dochakada]

arrive; reach

To reach a destination.

past : 도착하 + 였어요 → 도착했어요
present : 도착하 + 여요 → 도착해요
future : 도착하 + ㄹ 거예요 → 도착할 거예요

(224) 막히다 [makida]

be jammed

For cars to not run easily because there are many cars on the road.

past : 막히 + 었어요 → 막혔어요
present : 막히 + 어요 → 막혀요
future : 막히 + ㄹ 거예요 → 막힐 거예요

(225) 안전하다 [anjeonhada]

safe

Having no worry of falling into danger or becoming the victim of an accident.

past : 안전하 + 였어요 → **안전했어요**
present : 안전하 + 여요 → **안전해요**
future : 안전하 + ㄹ 거예요 → **안전할 거예요**

(226) 운전하다 [unjeonhada]

drive; operate

To move and handle a machine or car.

past : 운전하 + 였어요 → **운전했어요**
present : 운전하 + 여요 → **운전해요**
future : 운전하 + ㄹ 거예요 → **운전할 거예요**

(227) 위험하다 [wiheomhada]

dangerous; risky

Not safe due to the possibility of being harmed or injured.

past : 위험하 + 였어요 → **위험했어요**
present : 위험하 + 여요 → **위험해요**
future : 위험하 + ㄹ 거예요 → **위험할 거예요**

(228) 주차하다 [juchahada]

park

To keep a car at a certain space.

past : 주차하 + 였어요 → **주차했어요**
present : 주차하 + 여요 → **주차해요**
future : 주차하 + ㄹ 거예요 → **주차할 거예요**

(229) 출발하다 [chulbalhada]

depart; leave

To leave a place, heading for another place.

past : 출발하 + 였어요 → **출발했어요**
present : 출발하 + 여요 → **출발해요**
future : 출발하 + ㄹ 거예요 → **출발할 거예요**

(230) 타다 [tada]

ride; get on; board

To mount a vehicle or the body of an animal used as a vehicle.

past : 타 + 았어요 → **탔어요**
present : 타 + 아요 → **타요**
future : 타 + ㄹ 거예요 → **탈 거예요**

(231) 출근하다 [chulgeunhada]

go to work; arrive at work

To leave home for a workplace or to arrive at a workplace, to work.

past : 출근하 + 였어요 → **출근했어요**
present : 출근하 + 여요 → **출근해요**
future : 출근하 + ㄹ 거예요 → **출근할 거예요**

(232) 출퇴근하다 [chultoegeunhada]

commute

To go to work or leave work.

past : 출퇴근하 + 였어요 → **출퇴근했어요**
present : 출퇴근하 + 여요 → **출퇴근해요**
future : 출퇴근하 + ㄹ 거예요 → **출퇴근할 거예요**

(233) 취직하다 [chwijikada]
get a job; be hired; be employed
To obtain a job and go to work.

past : 취직하 + 였어요 → 취직했어요
present : 취직하 + 여요 → 취직해요
future : 취직하 + ㄹ 거예요 → 취직할 거예요

(234) 퇴근하다 [toegeunhada]
leaving work; arriving home from work
An act of leaving one's workplace or returning home after work.

past : 퇴근하 + 였어요 → 퇴근했어요
present : 퇴근하 + 여요 → 퇴근해요
future : 퇴근하 + ㄹ 거예요 → 퇴근할 거예요

(235) 회의하다 [hoeuihada]
hold a meeting; have a conference
For people to gather and discuss a topic, issue, etc.

past : 회의하 + 였어요 → 회의했어요
present : 회의하 + 여요 → 회의해요
future : 회의하 + ㄹ 거예요 → 회의할 거예요

(236) 거짓말하다 [geojinmalhada]
lie; tell a lie
To say something untrue as if it were true.

past : 거짓말하 + 였어요 → 거짓말했어요
present : 거짓말하 + 여요 → 거짓말해요
future : 거짓말하 + ㄹ 거예요 → 거짓말할 거예요

(237) 농담하다 [nongdamhada]

joke

To say to make fun of someone or make people laugh.

past : 농담하 + 였어요 → **농담했어요**
present : 농담하 + 여요 → **농담해요**
future : 농담하 + ㄹ 거예요 → **농담할 거예요**

(238) 대답하다 [daedapada]

answer; reply

To reply to a call.

past : 대답하 + 였어요 → **대답했어요**
present : 대답하 + 여요 → **대답해요**
future : 대답하 + ㄹ 거예요 → **대답할 거예요**

(239) 대화하다 [daehwahada]

talk

To have a conversation face to face.

past : 대화하 + 였어요 → **했어요**
present : 대화하 + 여요 → **해요**
future : 대화하 + ㄹ 거예요 → **할 거예요**

(240) 드리다 [deurida]

say; say hello

To say something or to greet an elder.

past : 드리 + 었어요 → **드렸어요**
present : 드리 + 어요 → **드려요**
future : 드리 + ㄹ 거예요 → **드릴 거예요**

(241) 말하다 [malhada]

say; tell; speak; talk

To verbally present a fact or one's thoughts or feelings.

past : 말하 + 였어요 → **말했어요**
present : 말하 + 여요 → **말해요**
future : 말하 + ㄹ 거예요 → **말할 거예요**

(242) 묻다 [mutda]

ask; inquire; interrogate

To say something, demanding an answer or explanation.

past : 묻 + 었어요 → **물었어요**
present : 묻 + 어요 → **물어요**
future : 묻 + 을 거예요 → **물을 거예요**

(243) 물어보다 [mureoboda]

ask; inquire; interrogate

To ask a question to find out something.

past : 물어보 + 았어요 → **물어봤어요**
present : 물어보 + 아요 → **물어봐요**
future : 물어보 + ㄹ 거예요 → **물어볼 거예요**

(244) 설명하다 [seolmyeonghada]

explain; account for

To describe something to another person in a way that he/she could understand easily.

past : 설명하 + 였어요 → **설명했어요**
present : 설명하 + 여요 → **설명해요**
future : 설명하 + ㄹ 거예요 → **설명할 거예요**

(245) 쓰다 [sseuda]

write

To write some letters by drawing strokes on paper with a writing instrument such as a pencil, pen, etc.

past : 쓰 + 었어요 → 썼어요
present : 쓰 + 어요 → 써요
future : 쓰 + ㄹ 거예요 → 쓸 거예요

(246) 얘기하다 [yaegihada]

tell; say; speak

To talk to someone about a certain fact, state, phenomenon, experience, thought, etc.

past : 얘기하 + 였어요 → 얘기했어요
present : 얘기하 + 여요 → 얘기해요
future : 얘기하 + ㄹ 거예요 → 얘기할 거예요

(247) 읽다 [ikda]

read; read out

To see written words or letters, and utter them as they are pronounced.

past : 읽 + 었어요 → 읽었어요
present : 읽 + 어요 → 읽어요
future : 읽 + 을 거예요 → 읽을 거예요

(248) 질문하다 [jilmunhada]

ask a question

To ask about something one does not know or wants to know.

past : 질문하 + 였어요 → 질문했어요
present : 질문하 + 여요 → 질문해요
future : 질문하 + ㄹ 거예요 → 질문할 거예요

(249) 칭찬하다 [chingchanhada]

praise; compliment

To express one's appreciation of someone's strength or achievement, etc.

past : 칭찬하 + 였어요 → 칭찬했어요
present : 칭찬하 + 여요 → 칭찬해요
future : 칭찬하 + ㄹ 거예요 → 칭찬할 거예요

(250) 끊다 [kkeunta]

hang up

To stop exchanging words or thoughts through the telephone or Internet.

past : 끊 + 었어요 → 끊었어요
present : 끊 + 어요 → 끊어요
future : 끊 + 을 거예요 → 끊을 거예요

(251) 부치다 [buchida]

send

To forward a letter, object, etc.

past : 부치 + 었어요 → 부쳤어요
present : 부치 + 어요 → 부쳐요
future : 부치 + ㄹ 거예요 → 부칠 거예요

(252) 줄이다 [jurida]

turn down; reduce; shorten

To make the length, area, volume, etc., of an object smaller than original.

past : 줄이 + 었어요 → 줄였어요
present : 줄이 + 어요 → 줄여요
future : 줄이 + ㄹ 거예요 → 줄일 거예요

(253) 줄다 [julda]

shrink; diminish

For an object's length, area, volume, etc. to become smaller than the original.

past : 줄 + 었어요 → 줄었어요
present : 줄 + 어요 → 줄어요
future : 줄 + ㄹ 거예요 → 줄 거예요

(254) 비다 [bida]

be empty; be vacant

For a space to contain nothing or no one.

past : 비 + 었어요 → 비었어요
present : 비 + 어요 → 비어요
future : 비 + ㄹ 거예요 → 빌 거예요

(255) 모자라다 [mojarada]

lack; be short; be insufficient

To not reach a fixed number, quantity, or level.

past : 모자라 + 았어요 → 모자랐어요
present : 모자라 + 아요 → 모자라요
future : 모자라 + ㄹ 거예요 → 모자랄 거예요

(256) 늘다 [neulda]

be extended

For the length, area, volume, etc., of something to become longer or bigger than before.

past : 늘 + 었어요 → 늘었어요
present : 늘 + 어요 → 늘어요
future : 늘 + ㄹ 거예요 → 늘 거예요

(257) 남다 [namda]

remain; be left

For part of something to remain without being used up.

past : 남 + 았어요 → 남았어요
present : 남 + 아요 → 남아요
future : 남 + 을 거예요 → 남을 거예요

(258) 남기다 [namgida]

leave

To leave part of something without using it up.

past : 남기 + 었어요 → 남겼어요
present : 남기 + 어요 → 남겨요
future : 남기 + ㄹ 거예요 → 남길 거예요

(259) 오다 [oda]

come; arrive

For the rain, snow, etc., to fall, or for a cold spell to arrive.

past : 오 + 았어요 → 왔어요
present : 오 + 아요 → 와요
future : 오 + ㄹ 거예요 → 올 거예요

(260) 불다 [bulda]

blow

For a wind to form and move in a certain direction.

past : 불 + 었어요 → 불었어요
present : 불 + 어요 → 불어요
future : 불 + ㄹ 거예요 → 불 거예요

(261) 내리다 [naerida]

fall; descend

To snow, rain, etc.

past : 내리 + 었어요 → 내렸어요
present : 내리 + 어요 → 내려요
future : 내리 + ㄹ 거예요 → 내릴 거예요

(262) 그치다 [geuchida]

stop

For a continuing matter, movement, phenomenon, etc., to cease.

past : 그치 + 었어요 → 그쳤어요
present : 그치 + 어요 → 그쳐요
future : 그치 + ㄹ 거예요 → 그칠 거예요

(263) 배우다 [baeuda]

learn

To obtain new knowledge.

past : 배우 + 었어요 → 배웠어요
present : 배우 + 어요 → 배워요
future : 배우 + ㄹ 거예요 → 배울 거예요

(264) 가르치다 [gareuchida]

teach; instruct

To explain knowledge or skills to help someone understand it.

past : 가르치 + 었어요 → 가르쳤어요
present : 가르치 + 어요 → 가르쳐요
future : 가르치 + ㄹ 거예요 → 가르칠 거예요

(265) 팔다 [palda]

sell

To give an object or a right to someone or provide one's effort, etc., to someone after receiving money for it.

past : 팔 + 았어요 → 팔았어요
present : 팔 + 아요 → 팔아요
future : 팔 + ㄹ 거예요 → 팔 거예요

(266) 팔리다 [pallida]

be sold

For an object or a right to be given to someone or for one's effort, etc., to be provided to someone after money is received for it.

past : 팔리 + 었어요 → 팔렸어요
present : 팔리 + 어요 → 팔려요
future : 팔리 + ㄹ 거예요 → 파릴 거예요

(267) 올리다 [ollida]

increase; raise

To make a price, figure, energy, etc., get higher or increase.

past : 올리 + 었어요 → 올렸어요
present : 올리 + 어요 → 올려요
future : 올리 + ㄹ 거예요 → 올릴 거예요

(268) 사다 [sada]

buy; purchase; get

To get ownership of an item, right, etc., by paying for it.

past : 사 + 았어요 → 샀어요
present : 사 + 아요 → 사요
future : 사 + ㄹ 거예요 → 살 거예요

(269) 빌리다 [billida]

borrow; rent

To borrow goods, money, etc., from someone for a certain period of time on the condition of returning them or paying a price later.

past : 빌리 + 었어요 → **빌렸어요**
present : 빌리 + 어요 → **빌려요**
future : 빌리 + ㄹ 거예요 → **빌릴 거예요**

(270) 벌다 [beolda]

make; earn

To obtain or save money by doing some work.

past : 벌 + 었어요 → **벌었어요**
present : 벌 + 어요 → **벌어요**
future : 벌 + ㄹ 거예요 → **벌 거예요**

(271) 들다 [deulda]

be spent; be used; be poured; be invested

For money, time, efforts, etc., to be used for something.

past : 들 + 었어요 → **들었어요**
present : 들 + 어요 → **들어요**
future : 들 + ㄹ 거예요 → **들 거예요**

(272) 깎다 [kkakda]

lower

To decrease the price, amount, degree, etc. of something.

past : 깎 + 았어요 → **깎았어요**
present : 깎 + 아요 → **깎아요**
future : 깎 + 을 거예요 → **깎을 거예요**

(273) 갚다 [gapda]

pay back; repay

To return what one borrows.

past : 갚 + 았어요 → 갚았어요
present : 갚 + 아요 → 갚아요
future : 갚 + 을 거예요 → 갚을 거예요

(274) 통화하다 [tonghwahada]

talk over the telephone

To talk with someone using a telephone.

past : 통화하 + 였어요 → 통화했어요
present : 통화하 + 여요 → 통화해요
future : 통화하 + ㄹ 거예요 → 통화할 거예요

(275) 교환하다 [gyohwanhada]

change

To change one thing for another.

past : 교환하 + 였어요 → 교환했어요
present : 교환하 + 여요 → 교환해요
future : 교환하 + ㄹ 거예요 → 교환할 거예요

(276) 배달하다 [baedalhada]

deliver

To deliver mail, goods, food, etc.

past : 배달하 + 였어요 → 배달했어요
present : 배달하 + 여요 → 배달해요
future : 배달하 + ㄹ 거예요 → 배달할 거예요

(277) 선택하다 [seontaekada]

choose; make a choice; select

To choose what one needs among many.

past : 선택하 + 였어요 → **선택했어요**
present : 선택하 + 여요 → **선택해요**
future : 선택하 + ㄹ 거예요 → **선택할 거예요**

(278) 할인하다 [harinhada]

give a discount; reduce

To subtract a certain amount of money from the original price.

past : 할인하 + 였어요 → **할인했어요**
present : 할인하 + 여요 → **할인해요**
future : 할인하 + ㄹ 거예요 → **할인할 거예요**

(279) 환전하다 [hwanjeonhada]

change; exchange

To exchange the currency of a country for another country's currency.

past : 환전하 + 였어요 → **환전했어요**
present : 환전하 + 여요 → **환전해요**
future : 환전하 + ㄹ 거예요 → **환전할 거예요**

(280) 결석하다 [gyeolseokada]

be absent from; stay away from

To miss official gatherings, such as school or meetings.

past : 결석하 + 였어요 → **결석했어요**
present : 결석하 + 여요 → **결석해요**
future : 결석하 + ㄹ 거예요 → **결석할 거예요**

(281) 공부하다 [gongbuhada]

study

To gain knowledge by learning studies or techniques.

past : 공부하 + 였어요 → 공부했어요
present : 공부하 + 여요 → 공부해요
future : 공부하 + ㄹ 거예요 → 공부할 거예요

(282) 교육하다 [gyoyukada]

educate; train

To teach knowledge, culture, techniques, etc., in order to enhance a person's ability.

past : 교육하 + 였어요 → 교육했어요
present : 교육하 + 여요 → 교육해요
future : 교육하 + ㄹ 거예요 → 교육할 거예요

(283) 복습하다 [bokseupada]

review

To go over what has been learned.

past : 복습하 + 였어요 → 복습했어요
present : 복습하 + 여요 → 복습해요
future : 복습하 + ㄹ 거예요 → 복습할 거예요

(284) 숙제하다 [sukjehada]

do one's homework

To do the assignment given to students to do after class as a review or preview.

past : 숙제하 + 였어요 → 숙제했어요
present : 숙제하 + 여요 → 숙제해요
future : 숙제하 + ㄹ 거예요 → 숙제할 거예요

(285) 연습하다 [yeonseupada]

practice; rehearse

To make oneself familiar with something by doing it repeatedly as if in a real situation.

past : 연습하 + 였어요 → **연습했어요**
present : 연습하 + 여요 → **연습해요**
future : 연습하 + ㄹ 거예요 → **연습할 거예요**

(286) 예습하다 [yeseupada]

study in advance

To study in advance for the next class.

past : 예습하 + 였어요 → **예습했어요**
present : 예습하 + 여요 → **예습해요**
future : 예습하 + ㄹ 거예요 → **예습할 거예요**

(287) 입학하다 [ipakada]

be enrolled at a school; enter a school

To enter a school to study as a student.

past : 입학하 + 였어요 → **입학했어요**
present : 입학하 + 여요 → **입학해요**
future : 입학하 + ㄹ 거예요 → **입학할 거예요**

(288) 졸업하다 [joreopada]

graduate

For a student to complete all the courses required by a school.

past : 졸업하 + 였어요 → **졸업했어요**
present : 졸업하 + 여요 → **졸업해요**
future : 졸업하 + ㄹ 거예요 → **졸업할 거예요**

(289) 지각하다 [jigakada]

be late

To go to work or school later than the set time.

past : 지각하 + 였어요 → **지각했어요**
present : 지각하 + 여요 → **지각해요**
future : 지각하 + ㄹ 거예요 → **지각할 거예요**

(290) 출석하다 [chulseokada]

attend

To go to a class, meeting, etc., and be there.

past : 출석하 + 였어요 → **출석했어요**
present : 출석하 + 여요 → **출석해요**
future : 출석하 + ㄹ 거예요 → **출석할 거예요**

한국어(Korean)

형용사(adjective) 137

(1) 고프다 [gopeuda]

hungry

Wanting to eat food due to an empty stomach.

배가 <u>고파요</u>.

baega gopayo.

배+가 <u>고프(고프)+아요</u>.
        <u>고파요</u>

배 : stomach; belly

가 : A postpositional particle referring to a subject under a certain state or situation, or the subject of an act.

고프다 : hungry

-아요 : (informal addressee-raising) A sentence-final ending used to describe a certain fact, ask a question, give an order, or advise. <description>

(2) 부르다 [bureuda]

full

Feeling one's stomach is stuffed after eating food.

배가 <u>불러요</u>.

baega bulleoyo.

배+가 <u>부르(불ㄹ)+어요</u>.
        <u>불러요</u>

배 : stomach; belly

가 : A postpositional particle referring to a subject under a certain state or situation, or the subject of an act.

부르다 : full

-어요 : (informal addressee-raising) A sentence-final ending used to describe a certain fact, ask a question, give an order, or advise. <description>

(3) 아프다 [apeuda]

hurting; aching

Feeling pain or suffering due to an injury or illness.

목이 아파요.

mogi apayo.

목+이 아프(아파)+아요.
　　　　아파요

목 : neck

이 : A postpositional particle referring to a subject under a certain state or situation, or the agent of an action.

아프다 : hurting; aching

-아요 : (informal addressee-raising) A sentence-final ending used to describe a certain fact, ask a question, give an order, or advise. <description>

(4) 고맙다 [gomapda]

thankful; grateful

Pleased and wanting to return a favor to someone.

도와줘서 고마워요.

dowajwoseo gomawoyo.

도와주+어서 고맙(고마우)+어요.
　　　　　　고마워요

도와주다 : help; assist

-어서 : A connective ending used for a reason or cause.

고맙다 : thankful; grateful

-어요 : (informal addressee-raising) A sentence-final ending used to describe a certain fact, ask a question, give an order, or advise. <description>

(5) 괜찮다 [gwaenchanta]

nice; fine

Fairly good.

맛이 <u>괜찮아요</u>.

masi gwaenchanayo.

맛+이 괜찮+아요.

맛 : taste

이 : A postpositional particle referring to a subject under a certain state or situation, or the agent of an action.

괜찮다 : nice; fine

-아요 : (informal addressee-raising) A sentence-final ending used to describe a certain fact, ask a question, give an order, or advise. <description>

(6) 귀엽다 [gwiyeopda]

cute; adorable; sweet

Pretty and adorable.

얼굴이 <u>귀여워요</u>.

eolguri gwiyeowoyo.

얼굴+이 <u>귀엽(귀여우)+어요</u>.
　　　　　　귀여워요

얼굴 : face

이 : A postpositional particle referring to a subject under a certain state or situation, or the agent of an action.

귀엽다 : cute; adorable; sweet

-어요 : (informal addressee-raising) A sentence-final ending used to describe a certain fact, ask a question, give an order, or advise. <description>

(7) 귀찮다 [gwichanta]

feel annoyed

Disliking and feeling tired of doing something.

씻기가 <u>귀찮아요</u>.

ssitgiga gwichanayo.

씻+기+가 귀찮+아요.

씻다 : wash
-기 : An ending of a word used to make the preceding word function as a noun.
가 : A postpositional particle referring to a subject under a certain state or situation, or the subject of an act.
귀찮다 : feel annoyed
-아요 : (informal addressee-raising) A sentence-final ending used to describe a certain fact, ask a question, give an order, or advise. <description>

(8) 그립다 [geuripda]

miss

Wanting to see and meet someone very much.

가족이 <u>그리워요</u>.

gajogi geuriwoyo.

가족+이 <u>그립(그리우)+어요</u>.
　　　　　　그리워요

가족 : family
이 : A postpositional particle referring to a subject under a certain state or situation, or the agent of an action.
그립다 : miss
-어요 : (informal addressee-raising) A sentence-final ending used to describe a certain fact, ask a question, give an order, or advise. <description>

(9) 기쁘다 [gippeuda]

happy; glad

Feeling very good and in a good mood.

시험에 합격해서 <u>기뻐요</u>.

siheome hapgyeokaeseo gippeoyo.

시험+에 합격하+여서 <u>기쁘(기ㅃ)+어요</u>.

　　　　　　　　　　기뻐요

시험 : test; exam

에 : A postpositional particle to indicate that the preceding statement is the subject that is influenced by a certain action, emotion, etc.

합격하다 : pass; get through

-여서 : A connective ending used to indicate a reason or cause.

기쁘다 : happy; glad

-어요 : (informal addressee-raising) A sentence-final ending used to describe a certain fact, ask a question, give an order, or advise. <description>

(10) 답답하다 [dapdapada]

stifling; suffocating

Feeling stifled or hard to breathe.

가슴이 <u>답답해요</u>.

gaseumi dapdapaeyo.

가슴+이 <u>답답하+여요</u>.

　　　　　답답해요

가슴 : heart; lungs

이 : A postpositional particle referring to a subject under a certain state or situation, or the agent of an action.

답답하다 : stifling; suffocating

-여요 : (informal addressee-raising) A sentence-final ending used to describe a certain fact, ask a question, give an order, or advise. <description>

(11) 무섭다 [museopda]

fearful; scared of

Feeling scared of something, or feeling afraid something might happen.

귀신이 <u>무서워요</u>.

gwisini museowoyo.

귀신+이 <u>무섭(무서우)+어요</u>.
　　　　　 무서워요

귀신 : deity; god

이 : A postpositional particle referring to a subject under a certain state or situation, or the agent of an action.

무섭다 : fearful; scared of

-어요 : (informal addressee-raising) A sentence-final ending used to describe a certain fact, ask a question, give an order, or advise. <description>

(12) 반갑다 [bangapda]

glad; joyful

Joyful and happy as one meets a person that one missed.

만나게 되어 <u>반가워요</u>.

mannage doeeo bangawoyo.

만나+[게 되]+어 <u>반갑(반가우)+어요</u>.
　　　　　　　　　 반가워요

만나다 : meet; meet with; join

-게 되다 : An expression used to indicate that something will become the state or situation mentioned in the preceding statement.

-어 : A connective ending used when the preceding statement is the cause or reason for the following statement.

반갑다 : glad; joyful

-어요 : (informal addressee-raising) A sentence-final ending used to describe a certain fact, ask a question, give an order, or advise. <description>

(13) 부끄럽다 [bukkeureopda]

shy

Bashful or coy.

칭찬해 주시니 <u>부끄러워요</u>.

chingchanhae jusini bukkeureowoyo.

<u>칭찬하</u>+[여 주]+<u>시</u>+니 <u>부끄럽(부끄러우)+어요</u>.
     칭찬해 주시니   부끄러워요

칭찬하다 : praise; compliment
-여 주다 : An expression used to indicate that one does the act mentioned in the preceding statement for someone.
-시- : An ending of a word used for the subject honorifics of an action or state.
-니 : A connective ending used when the preceding statement is the cause, reason, or premise for the following statement.
부끄럽다 : shy
-어요 : (informal addressee-raising) A sentence-final ending used to describe a certain fact, ask a question, give an order, or advise. <description>

(14) 부럽다 [bureopda]

envious of

Desiring to achieve or possess the same kind of feat or thing that others have achieved or possess because they look good.

한국어 잘하는 사람이 <u>부러워요</u>.

hangugeo jalhaneun sarami bureowoyo.

한국어 잘하+는 사람+이 <u>부럽(부러우)+어요</u>.
                          부러워요

한국어 : Korean; Korean language
잘하다 : be skillful; be expert; be good
-는 : An ending of a word that makes the preceding statement function as an adnominal phrase and implies that an event or action is happening in the present.
사람 : human; man

이 : A postpositional particle referring to a subject under a certain state or situation, or the agent of an action.

부럽다 : envious of

-어요 : (informal addressee-raising) A sentence-final ending used to describe a certain fact, ask a question, give an order, or advise. <description>

(15) 불쌍하다 [bulssanghada]

pitiful; pathetic

Feeling sorry and sad because someone is in a bad situation.

주인을 잃은 강아지가 불쌍해요.

juineul ireun gangajiga bulssanghaeyo.

주인+을 잃+은 강아지+가 불쌍하+여요.
불쌍해요

주인 : owner

을 : A postpositional particle used to indicate the subject that an action has a direct influence on.

잃다 : be deprived of; be bereft of; lose

-은 : An ending of word that makes the preceding word function as an adnominal phrase and implies that an action has been completed and its state continues.

강아지 : puppy

가 : A postpositional particle referring to a subject under a certain state or situation, or the subject of an act.

불쌍하다 : pitiful; pathetic

-여요 : (informal addressee-raising) A sentence-final ending used to describe a certain fact, ask a question, give an order, or advise. <description>

(16) 섭섭하다 [seopseopada]

sorry; regrettable

Sorry and feeling the lack of someone or something.

선생님과 헤어지기가 섭섭해요.

seonsaengnimgwa heeojigiga seopseopaeyo.

선생님+과 헤어지+기+가 섭섭하+여요.
섭섭해요

선생님 : teacher; master

과 : A postpositional word referring to the person when doing something with him/her.

헤어지다 : part; bid farewell; say good-bye

-기 : An ending of a word used to make the preceding word function as a noun.

가 : A postpositional particle referring to a subject under a certain state or situation, or the subject of an act.

섭섭하다 : sorry; regrettable

-여요 : (informal addressee-raising) A sentence-final ending used to describe a certain fact, ask a question, give an order, or advise. <description>

(17) 소중하다 [sojunghada]

valuable

Very precious.

가족이 가장 소중해요.

gajogi gajang sojunghaeyo.

가족+이 가장 소중하+여요.
　　　　　　　소중해요

가족 : family

이 : A postpositional particle referring to a subject under a certain state or situation, or the agent of an action.

가장 : best

소중하다 : valuable

-여요 : (informal addressee-raising) A sentence-final ending used to describe a certain fact, ask a question, give an order, or advise. <description>

(18) 슬프다 [seulpeuda]

sad

Sad and sorrowful enough to make one cry.

영화의 내용이 슬퍼요.

yeonghwae naeyongi seulpeoyo.

영화+의 내용+이 슬프(슬프)+어요.
　　　　　　　슬퍼요

영화 : film; movie

의 : A postpositional particle used to indicate that the referent of the following word is owned by, belongs to, is related to, originates from, or is the object of what the preceding word indicates.

내용 : story; message

이 : A postpositional particle referring to a subject under a certain state or situation, or the agent of an action.

슬프다 : sad

-어요 : (informal addressee-raising) A sentence-final ending used to describe a certain fact, ask a question, give an order, or advise. <description>

(19) 시원하다 [siwonhada]

cool

Moderately cool, neither hot nor cold.

바람이 <u>시원해요</u>.

barami siwonhaeyo.

바람+이 <u>시원하+여요</u>.
　　　　　시원해요

바람 : wind

이 : A postpositional particle referring to a subject under a certain state or situation, or the agent of an action.

시원하다 : cool

-여요 : (informal addressee-raising) A sentence-final ending used to describe a certain fact, ask a question, give an order, or advise. <description>

(20) 싫다 [silta]

disgusting; distasteful; having no taste for

Being not to one's taste

매운 음식이 <u>싫어요</u>.

maeun eumsigi sireoyo.

<u>맵(매우)+ㄴ</u> 음식+이 싫+어요.
　매운

맵다 : spicy; hot

-ㄴ : An ending of a word that makes the preceding statement function as an adnominal phrase and refers to the present state.

음식 : food

이 : A postpositional particle referring to a subject under a certain state or situation, or the agent of an action.

싫다 : disgusting; distasteful; having no taste for

-어요 : (informal addressee-raising) A sentence-final ending used to describe a certain fact, ask a question, give an order, or advise. <description>

(21) 외롭다 [oeropda]

lonely; solitary

Being lonesome because one is alone or has nobody to depend on.

지금 몹시 외로워요.

jigeum mopsi oerowoyo.

지금 몹시 외롭(외로우)+어요.
　　　　　외로워요

지금 : now; immediately

몹시 : much; extremely

외롭다 : lonely; solitary

-어요 : (informal addressee-raising) A sentence-final ending used to describe a certain fact, ask a question, give an order, or advise. <description>

(22) 좋다 [jota]

good; great; excellent

Excellent and satisfactory in features and content.

이 물건은 품질이 좋아요.

i mulgeoneun pumjiri joayo.

이 물건+은 품질+이 좋+아요.

이 : this

물건 : article; thing; item; goods

은 : A postpositional particle used to indicate that a certain subject is the topic of a sentence.

품질 : quality

이 : A postpositional particle referring to a subject under a certain state or situation, or the agent of an action.

좋다 : good; great; excellent

-아요 : (informal addressee-raising) A sentence-final ending used to describe a certain fact, ask a question, give an order, or advise. <description>

(23) 죄송하다 [joesonghada]

sorry

Very sorry as if one committed a wrongdoing.

늦어서 죄송해요.

neujeoseo joesonghaeyo.

늦+어서 죄송하+여요.
        죄송해요

늦다 : be late

-어서 : A connective ending used for a reason or cause.

죄송하다 : sorry

-여요 : (informal addressee-raising) A sentence-final ending used to describe a certain fact, ask a question, give an order, or advise. <description>

(24) 즐겁다 [jeulgeopda]

joyful; pleasant

Pleased and satisfied with something.

여행은 언제나 즐거워요.

yeohaengeun eonjena jeulgeowoyo.

여행+은 언제나 즐겁(즐거우)+어요.
            즐거워요

여행 : travel; trip
은 : A postpositional particle used to indicate that a certain subject is the topic of a sentence.
언제나 : always; all the time
즐겁다 : joyful; pleasant
-어요 : (informal addressee-raising) A sentence-final ending used to describe a certain fact, ask a question, give an order, or advise. <description>

(25) 급하다 [geupada]

urgent

Having to do something quickly.

갑자기 급한 일이 생겼어요.
gapjagi geupan iri saenggyeosseoyo.

갑자기 급하+ㄴ 일+이 생기+었+어요.
　　　　급한　　　　　　생겼어요

갑자기 : suddenly; all of a sudden
급하다 : urgent
-ㄴ : An ending of a word that makes the preceding statement function as an adnominal phrase and refers to the present state.
일 : business; engagement
이 : A postpositional particle referring to a subject under a certain state or situation, or the agent of an action.
생기다 : occur; take place
-었- : An ending of a word used to indicate that an event was completed in the past or its result continues in the present.
-어요 : (informal addressee-raising) A sentence-final ending used to describe a certain fact, ask a question, give an order, or advise. <description>

(26) 조용하다 [joyonghada]

quiet

Restrained in speech and gentle in behavior.

도서관에서는 조용하게 말하세요.
doseogwaneseoneun joyonghage malhaseyo.

도서관+에서+는 조용하+게 말하+세요.

도서관 : library

에서 : A postpositional particle used to indicate that the preceding word refers to a place where a certain action is being done.

는 : A postpositional particle used to indicate that a certain subject is the topic of a sentence.

조용하다 : quiet

-게 : A connective ending used when the preceding statement is the purpose, result, method, amount, etc., of something mentioned in the following statement.

말하다 : say; tell; speak; talk

-세요 : (informal addressee-raising) A sentence-final ending used to describe, ask a question, order, and request. <order>

(27) 곧다 [gotda]

straight; upright; direct

A road, line, posture, etc., being straight, not bent.

허리를 곧게 펴세요.

heorireul gotge pyeoseyo.

허리+를 곧+게 펴+세요.

허리 : waist

를 : A postpositional particle used to indicate the subject that an act has a direct influence on.

곧다 : straight; upright; direct

-게 : A connective ending used when the preceding statement is the purpose, result, method, amount, etc., of something mentioned in the following statement.

펴다 : stretch; stand tall

-세요 : (informal addressee-raising) A sentence-final ending used to describe, ask a question, order, and request. <order>

(28) 까다롭다 [kkadaropda]

complex; intricate

Difficult to handle due to complicated and strict conditions and methods.

이 문제는 <u>까다로워요</u>.

i munjeneun kkadarowoyo.

이 문제+는 <u>까다롭(까다로우)+어요</u>.
　　　　　　까따로워요

이 : this
문제 : problem; question
는 : A postpositional particle used to indicate that a certain subject is the topic of a sentence.
까다롭다 : complex; intricate
-어요 : (informal addressee-raising) A sentence-final ending used to describe a certain fact, ask a question, give an order, or advise. <description>

(29) 깔끔하다 [kkalkkeumhada]
clean; neat

A person's appearance being tidy and clean.

방이 아주 <u>깔끔해요</u>.

bangi aju kkalkkeumhaeyo.

방+이 아주 <u>깔끔하+여요</u>.
　　　　　　깔끔해요

방 : room
이 : A postpositional particle referring to a subject under a certain state or situation, or the agent of an action.
아주 : very; so; extremely
깔끔하다 : clean; neat
-여요 : (informal addressee-raising) A sentence-final ending used to describe a certain fact, ask a question, give an order, or advise. <description>

(30) 냉정하다 [naengjeonghada]
cold; callous; indifferent

A person's attitude being cold without kindness.

성격이 <u>냉정해요</u>.

seonggyeogi naengjeonghaeyo.

성격+이 <u>냉정하+여요</u>.
          냉정해요

성격 : personality; character

이 : A postpositional particle referring to a subject under a certain state or situation, or the agent of an action.

냉정하다 : cold; callous; indifferent

-여요 : (informal addressee-raising) A sentence-final ending used to describe a certain fact, ask a question, give an order, or advise. <description>

(31) 너그럽다 [neogeureopda]

generous; charitable

Understanding others' situation and showing ample generosity.

마음이 <u>너그러워요</u>.

maeumi neogeureowoyo.

마음+이 <u>너그럽(너그러우)+어요</u>.
          너그러워요

마음 : mood; feeling

이 : A postpositional particle referring to a subject under a certain state or situation, or the agent of an action.

너그럽다 : generous; charitable

-어요 : (informal addressee-raising) A sentence-final ending used to describe a certain fact, ask a question, give an order, or advise. <description>

(32) 느긋하다 [neugeutada]

comfortable; relaxed; carefree

Keeping one's composure and not hurrying.

숙제를 끝내서 마음이 <u>느긋해요</u>.

sukjereul kkeunnaeseo maeumi neugeutaeyo.

숙제+를 <u>끝내</u>+<u>어서</u> 마음+이 <u>느긋하</u>+<u>여요</u>.
       끝내서   **느긋해요**

숙제 : homework

를 : A postpositional particle used to indicate the subject that an act has a direct influence on.

끝내다 : complete; finish

-어서 : A connective ending used for a reason or cause.

마음 : mood; feeling

이 : A postpositional particle referring to a subject under a certain state or situation, or the agent of an action.

느긋하다 : comfortable; relaxed; carefree

-여요 : (informal addressee-raising) A sentence-final ending used to describe a certain fact, ask a question, give an order, or advise. \<description\>

(33) 다정하다 [dajeonghada]

kind; friendly

Warm-hearted and affectionate.

아버지는 가족들에게 무척 <u>다정해요</u>.

abeojineun gajokdeurege mucheok dajeonghaeyo.

아버지+는 가족+들+에게 무척 <u>다정하</u>+<u>여요</u>.
                             다정해요

아버지 : father; male parent

는 : A postpositional particle used to indicate that a certain subject is the topic of a sentence.

가족 : family

들 : A suffix used to mean plural.

에게 : A postpositional particle referring to the subject that is influenced by a certain action.

무척 : very; extremely

다정하다 : kind; friendly

-여요 : (informal addressee-raising) A sentence-final ending used to describe a certain fact, ask a question, give an order, or advise. \<description\>

(34) 못되다 [motdoeda]

nasty; naughty

(for one's personality or behavior) Morally bad.

동생은 못된 버릇이 있어요.

dongsaengeun motdoen beoreusi isseoyo.

동생+은 못되+ㄴ 버릇+이 있+어요.
　　　　　　못된

동생 : brother; sister

은 : A postpositional particle used to indicate that a certain subject is the topic of a sentence.

못되다 : nasty; naughty

-ㄴ : An ending of a word that makes the preceding statement function as an adnominal phrase and refers to the present state.

버릇 : habit

이 : A postpositional particle referring to a subject under a certain state or situation, or the agent of an action.

있다 : Having a certain object, qualification, ability, etc.

-어요 : (informal addressee-raising) A sentence-final ending used to describe a certain fact, ask a question, give an order, or advise. <description>

(35) 변덕스럽다 [byeondeokseureopda]

whimsical; changeable; inconstant

Words, behavior, feelings, etc., often changing capriciously.

요즘 날씨가 변덕스러워요.

yojeum nalssiga byeondeokseureowoyo.

요즘 날씨+가 변덕스럽(변덕스러우)+어요.
　　　　　　변덕스러워요

요즘 : nowadays; these days

날씨 : weather

가 : A postpositional particle referring to a subject under a certain state or situation, or the subject of an act.

변덕스럽다 : whimsical; changeable; inconstant

-어요 : (informal addressee-raising) A sentence-final ending used to describe a certain fact, ask a question, give an order, or advise. <description>

(36) 솔직하다 [soljikada]

frank; honest

Not lying or manipulating.

묻는 말에 솔직하게 대답하세요.

munneun mare soljikage daedapaseyo.

묻+는 말+에 솔직하+게 대답하+세요.

묻다 : ask; inquire; interrogate
-는 : An ending of a word that makes the preceding statement function as an adnominal phrase and implies that an event or action is happening in the present.
말 : words
에 : A postpositional particle to indicate that the preceding statement is the subject that is influenced by a certain action, emotion, etc.
솔직하다 : frank; honest
-게 : A connective ending used when the preceding statement is the purpose, result, method, amount, etc., of something mentioned in the following statement.
대답하다 : answer
-세요 : (informal addressee-raising) A sentence-final ending used to describe, ask a question, order, and request. <order>

(37) 순수하다 [sunsuhada]

guileless; innocent

Not having selfish desires or evil thoughts.

순수하게 세상을 살고 싶어요.

sunsuhage sesangeul salgo sipeoyo.

순수하+게 세상+을 살+[고 싶]+어요.

순수하다 : guileless; innocent

-게 : A connective ending used when the preceding statement is the purpose, result, method, amount, etc., of something mentioned in the following statement.

세상 : world

을 : A postpositional particle used to indicate the subject that an action has a direct influence on.

살다 : live

-고 싶다 : An expression used to state that the speaker wants to do the act mentioned in the preceding statement.

-어요 : (informal addressee-raising) A sentence-final ending used to describe a certain fact, ask a question, give an order, or advise. <description>

(38) 순진하다 [sunjinhada]

innocent

Being genuine without being artificial.

그 사람은 어린아이처럼 순진해요.

geu sarameun eorinaicheoreom sunjinhaeyo.

그 사람+은 어린아이+처럼 순진하+여요.
순진해요

그 : that

사람 : human; man

은 : A postpositional particle used to indicate that a certain subject is the topic of a sentence.

어린아이 : child; kid

처럼 : A postpositional particle used when something is similar or identical to something else in shape or level.

순진하다 : innocent

-여요 : (informal addressee-raising) A sentence-final ending used to describe a certain fact, ask a question, give an order, or advise. <description>

(39) 순하다 [sunhada]

meek; mild; docile

One's personality, attitude, etc., being gentle and good.

아이가 성격이 순해요.

aiga seonggyeogi sunhaeyo.

아이+가 성격+이 <u>순하+여요</u>.
　　　　　　　　순해요

아이 : child; kid
가 : A postpositional particle referring to a subject under a certain state or situation, or the subject of an act.
성격 : personality; character
이 : A postpositional particle referring to a subject under a certain state or situation, or the agent of an action.
순하다 : meek; mild; docile
-여요 : (informal addressee-raising) A sentence-final ending used to describe a certain fact, ask a question, give an order, or advise. <description>

(40) 활발하다 [hwalbalhada]

lively; cheerful; outgoing; vigorous
Being full of life and energy.

나는 활발한 사람이 좋아요.
naneun hwalbalhan sarami joayo.

나+는 활발하+ㄴ 사람+이 좋+아요.
　　　　활발한

나 : I
는 : A postpositional particle used to indicate that a certain subject is the topic of a sentence.
활발하다 : lively; cheerful; outgoing; vigorous
-ㄴ : An ending of a word that makes the preceding statement function as an adnominal phrase and refers to the present state.
사람 : human; man
이 : A postpositional particle referring to a subject under a certain state or situation, or the agent of an action.
좋다 : fond of; in love with
-아요 : (informal addressee-raising) A sentence-final ending used to describe a certain fact, ask a question, give an order, or advise. <description>

(41) 게으르다 [geeureuda]

lazy

Acting slowly and hating to move or work.

게으른 사람은 성공하지 못해요.

geeureun sarameun seonggonghaji motaeyo.

게으르+ㄴ 사람+은 성공하+[지 못하]+여요.
   게으른   성공하지 못해요

게으르다 : lazy

-ㄴ : An ending of a word that makes the preceding statement function as an adnominal phrase and refers to the present state.

사람 : human; man

은 : A postpositional particle used to indicate that a certain subject is the topic of a sentence.

성공하다 : succeed

-지 못하다 : An expression used to indicate that the speaker cannot do the act mentioned in the preceding statement, or that things did not work out as the subject intended.

-여요 : (informal addressee-raising) A sentence-final ending used to describe a certain fact, ask a question, give an order, or advise. <description>

(42) 부지런하다 [bujireonhada]

diligent; industrious

Tending to work steadily without being idle.

부지런한 사람이 성공할 수 있어요.

bujireonhan sarami seonggonghal su isseoyo.

부지런하+ㄴ 사람+이 성공하+[ㄹ 수 있]+어요.
  부지런한   성공할 수 있어요

부지런하다 : diligent; industrious

-ㄴ : An ending of a word that makes the preceding statement function as an adnominal phrase and refers to the present state.

사람 : human; man

이 : A postpositional particle referring to a subject under a certain state or situation, or the agent of an action.

성공하다 : succeed

-ㄹ 수 있다 : An expression used to indicate that an act or state is possible.

-어요 : (informal addressee-raising) A sentence-final ending used to describe a certain fact, ask a question, give an order, or advise. <description>

(43) 착하다 [chakada]

kind; generous

One's heart, behavior, etc., being honest, nice, and friendly.

그녀는 마음씨가 <u>착해요</u>.

geunyeoneun maeumssiga chakaeyo.

그녀+는 마음씨+가 <u>착하+여요</u>.
착해요

그녀 : she; her

는 : A postpositional particle used to indicate that a certain subject is the topic of a sentence.

마음씨 : temper

가 : A postpositional particle referring to a subject under a certain state or situation, or the subject of an act.

착하다 : kind; generous

-여요 : (informal addressee-raising) A sentence-final ending used to describe a certain fact, ask a question, give an order, or advise. <description>

(44) 친절하다 [chinjeolhada]

kind; hospitable

Treating someone gently and softly.

가게 주인은 모든 손님에게 <u>친절해요</u>.

gage juineun modeun sonnimege chinjeolhaeyo.

가게 주인+은 모든 손님+에게 <u>친절하+여요</u>.
친절해요

가게 : shop; store

주인 : owner

은 : A postpositional particle used to indicate that a certain subject is the topic of a sentence.
모든 : every
손님 : guest; customer
에게 : A postpositional particle referring to the subject that is influenced by a certain action.
친절하다 : kind; hospitable
-여요 : (informal addressee-raising) A sentence-final ending used to describe a certain fact, ask a question, give an order, or advise. <description>

(45) 날씬하다 [nalssinhada]

slender; svelte

A person's body being attractively slim and tall.

모델은 몸매가 <u>날씬해요</u>.

modereun mommaega nalssinhaeyo.

모델+은 몸매+가 <u>날씬하+여요</u>.
　　　　　　　　　날씬해요

모델 : model
은 : A postpositional particle used to indicate that a certain subject is the topic of a sentence.
몸매 : body figure; body shape
가 : A postpositional particle referring to a subject under a certain state or situation, or the subject of an act.
날씬하다 : slender; svelte
-여요 : (informal addressee-raising) A sentence-final ending used to describe a certain fact, ask a question, give an order, or advise. <description>

(46) 뚱뚱하다 [ttungttunghada]

fat; corpulent

A person's body being wide as a result of putting on weight.

요즘은 <u>뚱뚱한</u> 청소년이 많아졌어요.
yojeumeun ttungttunghan cheongsonyeoni manajeosseoyo.

요즘+은 뚱뚱하+ㄴ 청소년+이 <u>많아지+었+어요</u>.
　　　　　뚱뚱한　　　　　　　**많아졌어요**

요즘 : nowadays; these days

은 : A postpositional particle used to indicate that a certain subject is the topic of a sentence.

뚱뚱하다 : fat; corpulent

-ㄴ : An ending of a word that makes the preceding statement function as an adnominal phrase and refers to the present state.

청소년 : teenager

이 : A postpositional particle referring to a subject under a certain state or situation, or the agent of an action.

많아지다 : increase; grow

-었- : An ending of a word used to indicate that an event was completed in the past or its result continues in the present.

-어요 : (informal addressee-raising) A sentence-final ending used to describe a certain fact, ask a question, give an order, or advise. <description>

(47) 아름답다 [areumdapda]

beautiful; pretty

A color, appearance, or voice, etc., pleasing and satisfying one's eyes and ears.

여기 경치가 무척 <u>아름다워요</u>.
yeogi gyeongchiga mucheok areumdawoyo.

여기 경치+가 무척 <u>아름답(아름다우)</u>+어요.
아름다워요

여기 : here; this

경치 : scenery; scene; view

가 : A postpositional particle referring to a subject under a certain state or situation, or the subject of an act.

무척 : very; extremely

아름답다 : beautiful; pretty

-어요 : (informal addressee-raising) A sentence-final ending used to describe a certain fact, ask a question, give an order, or advise. <description>

(48) 어리다 [eorida]

young

Low in age.

내 동생은 아직 <u>어려요</u>.

nae dongsaengeun ajik eoryeoyo.

<u>나</u>+의 동생+은 아직 <u>어리</u>+어요.
　내　　　　　　　　어려요

나 : I

의 : A postpositional particle used to indicate that the referent of the following word is owned by, belongs to, is related to, originates from, or is the object of what the preceding word indicates.

동생 : brother; sister

은 : A postpositional particle used to indicate that a certain subject is the topic of a sentence.

아직 : yet; still

어리다 : young

-어요 : (informal addressee-raising) A sentence-final ending used to describe a certain fact, ask a question, give an order, or advise. <description>

(49) 예쁘다 [yeppeuda]

pretty; beautiful; comely

The appearance of someone or something looking good and beautiful.

구름이 참 <u>예뻐요</u>.

gureumi cham yeppeoyo.

구름+이 참 <u>예쁘(예ㅃ)</u>+어요.
　　　　　　예뻐요

구름 : cloud

이 : A postpositional particle referring to a subject under a certain state or situation, or the agent of an action.

참 : truly

예쁘다 : pretty; beautiful; comely

-어요 : (informal addressee-raising) A sentence-final ending used to describe a certain fact, ask a question, give an order, or advise. <description>

(50) 젊다 [jeomda]

young

Being in one's youthful years.

이 회사에는 <u>젊은</u> 사람들이 많아요.

i hoesaeneun jeolmeun saramdeuri manayo.

이 회사+에+는 젊+은 사람+들+이 많+아요.

이 : this

회사 : company; corporation

에 : A postpositional particle to indicate that the preceding statement refers to a certain place or space.

는 : A postpositional particle used to indicate that a certain subject is the topic of a sentence.

젊다 : young

-은 : An ending of a word that makes the preceding word function as an adnominal phrase and refers to the present state.

사람 : human; man

들 : A suffix used to mean plural.

이 : A postpositional particle referring to a subject under a certain state or situation, or the agent of an action.

많다 : plentiful; many; a lot of

-아요 : (informal addressee-raising) A sentence-final ending used to describe a certain fact, ask a question, give an order, or advise. <description>

(51) 똑똑하다 [ttokttokada]

clever; bright; sensible

Intelligent and wise.

친구는 <u>똑똑해서</u> 공부를 잘해요.

chinguneun ttokttokaeseo gongbureul jalhaeyo.

친구+는 <u>똑똑하+여서</u> 공부+를 <u>잘하+여요</u>.
　　　　　똑똑해서　　　　　　**잘해요**

친구 : friend

는 : A postpositional particle used to indicate that a certain subject is the topic of a sentence.

똑똑하다 : clever; bright; sensible

-여서 : A connective ending used to indicate a reason or cause.

공부 : study

를 : A postpositional particle used to indicate the subject that an act has a direct influence on.

잘하다 : be skillful; be expert; be good

-여요 : (informal addressee-raising) A sentence-final ending used to describe a certain fact, ask a question, give an order, or advise. <description>

(52) 못하다 [motada]

worse than; not as good as

The level or degree of something or someone not reaching that of others when compared.

음식 맛이 예전보다 못해요.

eumsik masi yejeonboda motaeyo.

음식 맛+이 예전+보다 못하+여요.
                    못해요

음식 : food
맛 : taste
이 : A postpositional particle referring to a subject under a certain state or situation, or the agent of an action.
예전 : past; old days
보다 : A postpositional particle that indicates the subject of a comparison when comparing different things.
못하다 : worse than; not as good as
-여요 : (informal addressee-raising) A sentence-final ending used to describe a certain fact, ask a question, give an order, or advise. <description>

(53) 쉽다 [swipda]

easy

Not hard or difficult to do.

시험 문제가 쉬웠어요.

siheom munjega swiwosseoyo.

시험 문제+가 쉽(쉬우)+었+어요.
                    쉬웠어요

시험 : test; exam
문제 : problem; question

가 : A postpositional particle referring to a subject under a certain state or situation, or the subject of an act.

쉽다 : easy

-었- : An ending of a word used to indicate that an event was completed in the past or its result continues in the present.

-어요 : (informal addressee-raising) A sentence-final ending used to describe a certain fact, ask a question, give an order, or advise. <description>

(54) 어렵다 [eoryeopda]

difficult; challenging

Very complicated or hard to do.

수학 문제는 항상 어려워요.

suhak munjeneun hangsang eoryeowoyo.

수학 문제+는 항상 어렵(어려우)+어요.
            어려워요

수학 : mathematics

문제 : problem; question

는 : A postpositional particle used to indicate that a certain subject is the topic of a sentence.

항상 : always; all the time

어렵다 : difficult; challenging

-어요 : (informal addressee-raising) A sentence-final ending used to describe a certain fact, ask a question, give an order, or advise. <description>

(55) 훌륭하다 [hullyunghada]

great; excellent; outstanding

Extremely good and excellent enough to be praised.

이 차의 성능은 훌륭해요.

i chae seongneungeun hullyunghaeyo.

이 차+의 성능+은 훌륭하+여요.
            훌륭해요

이 : this

차 : car; automobile; vehicle

의 : A postpositional particle used to indicate that the referent of the preceding word limits the properties or amount of the referent of the following word or that two words are on an equal footing.

성능 : performance; efficiency

은 : A postpositional particle used to indicate that a certain subject is the topic of a sentence.

훌륭하다 : great; excellent; outstanding

-여요 : (informal addressee-raising) A sentence-final ending used to describe a certain fact, ask a question, give an order, or advise. <description>

(56) 힘들다 [himdeulda]

strenuous; laborious

Requiring much power or effort.

이 동작은 너무 힘들어요.

i dongjageun neomu himdeureoyo.

이 동작+은 너무 힘들+어요.

이 : this

동작 : motion; movement

은 : A postpositional particle used to indicate that a certain subject is the topic of a sentence.

너무 : too

힘들다 : strenuous; laborious

-어요 : (informal addressee-raising) A sentence-final ending used to describe a certain fact, ask a question, give an order, or advise. <description>

(57) 궁금하다 [gunggeumhada]

curious

Having a strong desire to know about something.

무슨 화장품을 쓰는지 궁금해요?

museun hwajangpumeul sseuneunji gunggeumhaeyo?

무슨 화장품+을 쓰+는지 궁금하+여요?
                        궁금해요

무슨 : what

화장품 : cosmetics; makeup

을 : A postpositional particle used to indicate the subject that an action has a direct influence on.

쓰다 : use; work with; make use of

-는지 : A connective ending used to indicate an ambiguous reason or judgment about the following statement.

궁금하다 : curious

-여요 : (informal addressee-raising) A sentence-final ending used to describe a certain fact, ask a question, give an order, or advise. <question>

(58) 옳다 [olta]

right; righteous

Being in accord with a rule and just.

그는 평생 옳은 삶을 살아 왔어요.

geuneun pyeongsaeng oreun salmeul sara wasseoyo.

그+는 평생 옳+은 삶+을 살+[아 오]+았+어요.
살아 왔어요

그 : he

는 : A postpositional particle used to indicate that a certain subject is the topic of a sentence.

평생 : entire life

옳다 : right; righteous

-은 : An ending of a word that makes the preceding word function as an adnominal phrase and refers to the present state.

삶 : living

을 : A postpositional particle that indicates the noun object of the predicate.

살다 : live

-아 오다 : An expression used to indicate that the act or state mentioned in the preceding statement is continued as a certain set point of time is approaching.

-았- : An ending of a word used to indicate that an event was completed in the past or its result continues in the present.

-어요 : (informal addressee-raising) A sentence-final ending used to describe a certain fact, ask a question, give an order, or advise.<description>

(59) 바쁘다 [bappeuda]

busy; hectic

Having no time to do other things because one has many things to do or has little time.

식사를 못 할 정도로 <u>바빠요</u>.

siksareul mot hal jeongdoro bappayo.

식사+를 못 <u>하</u>+ㄹ 정도+로 <u>바쁘(바ㅃ)+아요</u>.
　　　　　할　　　　　　　　바빠요

식사 : meal

를 : A postpositional particle used to indicate the subject that an act has a direct influence on.

못 : not

하다 : do; drink; smoke

-ㄹ : An ending of a word that makes the preceding statement function as an adnominal phrase.

정도 : degree

로 : A postpositional particle that indicates a method or way to do something.

바쁘다 : busy; hectic

-아요 : (informal addressee-raising) A sentence-final ending used to describe a certain fact, ask a question, give an order, or advise.<description>

(60) 한가하다 [hangahada]

leisurely; unhurried; relaxed

Having time to spare without haste.

학교가 방학이어서 <u>한가해요</u>.

hakgyoga banghagieoseo hangahaeyo.

학교+가 방학+이+어서 <u>한가하+여요</u>.
　　　　　　　　　　　한가해요

학교 : school

가 : A postpositional particle referring to a subject under a certain state or situation, or the subject of an act.

방학 : vacation

이다 : A predicate particle indicating the meaning of the attribute or category of the thing that the subject of the sentence refers to.

-어서 : A connective ending used for a reason or cause.

한가하다 : leisurely; unhurried; relaxed

-여요 : (informal addressee-raising) A sentence-final ending used to describe a certain fact, ask a question, give an order, or advise.<description>

(61) 달다 [dalda]

sweet

Tasting like honey or sugar.

초콜릿이 너무 <u>달아요</u>.

chokollisi neomu darayo.

초콜릿+이 너무 달+아요.

초콜릿 : chocolate

이 : A postpositional particle referring to a subject under a certain state or situation, or the agent of an action.

너무 : too

달다 : sweet

-아요 : (informal addressee-raising) A sentence-final ending used to describe a certain fact, ask a question, give an order, or advise.<description>

(62) 맛없다 [madeopda]

ill-tasting; unsavory

The taste of food being not good.

배가 불러서 다 <u>맛없어요</u>.

baega bulleoseo da maseopseoyo.

배+가 <u>부르(불ㄹ)+어서</u> 다 맛없+어요.
　　　　 불러서

배 : stomach; belly

가 : A postpositional particle referring to a subject under a certain state or situation, or the subject of an act.

부르다 : full

-어서 : A connective ending used for a reason or cause.

다 : all; everything

맛없다 : ill-tasting; unsavory

-어요 : (informal addressee-raising) A sentence-final ending used to describe a certain fact, ask a question, give an order, or advise.<description>

(63) 맛있다 [maditda]

tasty; delicious

Tasting good.

어머니가 해 주신 음식이 제일 <u>맛있어요</u>.

eomeoniga hae jusin eumsigi jeil masisseoyo.

어머니+가 <u>하+[여 주]+시+ㄴ</u> 음식+이 제일 맛있+어요.
　　　　　　 해 주신

어머니 : mother

가 : A postpositional particle referring to a subject under a certain state or situation, or the subject of an act.

하다 : make

-여 주다 : An expression used to indicate that one does the act mentioned in the preceding statement for someone.

-시- : An ending of a word used for the subject honorifics of an action or state.

-ㄴ : An ending of a word that makes the preceding statement function as an adnominal phrase and indicates that an event or action has been completed and its state continues.

음식 : food

이 : A postpositional particle referring to a subject under a certain state or situation, or the agent of an action.

제일 : most

맛있다 : tasty; delicious

-어요 : (informal addressee-raising) A sentence-final ending used to describe a certain fact, ask a question, give an order, or advise.<description>

(64) 맵다 [maepda]

spicy; hot

Having a tangy taste like red peppers or mustard, which causes a sharp sensation at the tip of the tongue.

김치가 너무 <u>매워요</u>.

gimchiga neomu maewoyo.

김치+가 너무 <u>맵(매우)+어요</u>.
　　　　　　 매워요

김치 : A staple of the Korean diet made by salting vegetables such as kimchi cabbages, white radishes, etc., and seasoning and fermenting them.

가 : A postpositional particle referring to a subject under a certain state or situation, or the subject of an act.

너무 : too

맵다 : spicy; hot

-어요 : (informal addressee-raising) A sentence-final ending used to describe a certain fact, ask a question, give an order, or advise.<description>

(65) 시다 [sida]

sour

Tasting vinegary.

과일이 모두 <u>셔요</u>.

gwairi modu syeoyo.

과일+이 모두 <u>시+어요</u>.
　　　　　　　　셔요

과일 : fruit

이 : A postpositional particle referring to a subject under a certain state or situation, or the agent of an action.

모두 : all of

시다 : sour

-어요 : (informal addressee-raising) A sentence-final ending used to describe a certain fact, ask a question, give an order, or advise.<description>

(66) 시원하다 [siwonhada]

cool; hot

Food being cold and refreshing and thus it is good to eat, or being hot enough to make one feel refreshed.

국물이 <u>시원해요</u>.

gungmuri siwonhaeyo.

국물+이 <u>시원하+여요</u>.
　　　　　시원해요

국물 : broth, stock, or soup

이 : A postpositional particle referring to a subject under a certain state or situation, or the agent of an action.

시원하다 : cool; hot

-여요 : (informal addressee-raising) A sentence-final ending used to describe a certain fact, ask a question, give an order, or advise.<description>

(67) 싱겁다 [singgeopda]

not salty; flat

Not tasting salty enough.

찌개에 물을 넣어서 싱거워요.

jjigaee mureul neoeoseo singgeowoyo.

찌개+에 물+을 넣+어서 싱겁(싱거우)+어요.
싱거워요

찌개 : jjigae; stew

에 : A postpositional particle to indicate that the preceding statement is the subject to which a certain action or operation is applied.

물 : water

을 : A postpositional particle used to indicate the subject that an action has a direct influence on.

넣다 : add; mix

-어서 : A connective ending used for a reason or cause.

싱겁다 : not salty; flat

-어요 : (informal addressee-raising) A sentence-final ending used to describe a certain fact, ask a question, give an order, or advise.<description>

(68) 쓰다 [sseuda]

bitter

Tasting like medicine.

아이가 먹기에 약이 너무 써요.

aiga meokgie yagi neomu sseoyo.

아이+가 먹+기+에 약+이 너무 쓰(쓰)+어요.
써요

아이 : child; kid

가 : A postpositional particle referring to a subject under a certain state or situation, or the subject of an act.

먹다 : take; dose up with

-기 : An ending of a word used to make the preceding word function as a noun.

에 : A postpositional particle to indicate that the preceding statement is the condition, environment, state, etc., of something.

약 : medicine; medication; pill; drug

이 : A postpositional particle referring to a subject under a certain state or situation, or the agent of an action.

너무 : too

쓰다 : bitter

-어요 : (informal addressee-raising) A sentence-final ending used to describe a certain fact, ask a question, give an order, or advise.<description>

(69) 짜다 [jjada]

salty

Tasting like salt.

소금을 많이 넣어서 국물이 짜요.

sogeumeul mani neoeoseo gungmuri jjayo.

소금+을 많이 넣+어서 국물+이 짜+아요.

짜요

소금 : salt

을 : A postpositional particle used to indicate the subject that an action has a direct influence on.

많이 : much; in large numbers; in large amounts

넣다 : add; mix

-어서 : A connective ending used for a reason or cause.

국물 : broth, stock, or soup

이 : A postpositional particle referring to a subject under a certain state or situation, or the agent of an action.

짜다 : salty

-아요 : (informal addressee-raising) A sentence-final ending used to describe a certain fact, ask a question, give an order, or advise.<description>

(70) 깨끗하다 [kkaekkeutada]

clean

Not dirty.

화장실이 정말 <u>깨끗해요</u>.

hwajangsiri jeongmal kkaekkeutaeyo.

화장실+이 정말 <u>깨끗하+여요</u>.
　　　　　　　　　깨끗해요

화장실 : toilet; restroom; bathroom

이 : A postpositional particle referring to a subject under a certain state or situation, or the agent of an action.

정말 : really

깨끗하다 : clean

-여요 : (informal addressee-raising) A sentence-final ending used to describe a certain fact, ask a question, give an order, or advise.<description>

(71) 더럽다 [deoreopda]

dirty

Dirty or filthy due to dirt or residue.

차가 <u>더러워서</u> 세차를 했어요.

chaga deoreowoseo sechareul haesseoyo.

차+가 <u>더럽(더러우)+어서</u> 세차+를 <u>하+였+어요</u>.
　　　　더러워서　　　　　　　　　**했어요**

차 : car; automobile; vehicle

가 : A postpositional particle referring to a subject under a certain state or situation, or the subject of an act.

더럽다 : dirty

-어서 : A connective ending used for a reason or cause.

세차 : car wash

를 : A postpositional particle used to indicate the subject that an act has a direct influence on.

하다 : do; perform

-였- : An ending of a word used to indicate that an event was completed in the past or its result continues in the present.

-어요 : (informal addressee-raising) A sentence-final ending used to describe a certain fact, ask a question, give an order, or advise.<description>

(72) 불편하다 [bulpyeonhada]

inconvenient

Inconvenient to use something.

이곳은 교통이 불편해요.

igoseun gyotongi bulpyeonhaeyo.

이곳+은 교통+이 불편하+여요.
　　　　　　　　　 불편해요

이곳 : here
은 : A postpositional particle used to indicate that a certain subject is the topic of a sentence.
교통 : transportation; traffic
이 : A postpositional particle referring to a subject under a certain state or situation, or the agent of an action.
불편하다 : inconvenient
-여요 : (informal addressee-raising) A sentence-final ending used to describe a certain fact, ask a question, give an order, or advise.<description>

(73) 시끄럽다 [sikkeureopda]

loud

Unpleasantly loud and noisy.

시끄러운 소리가 들려요.

sikkeureoun soriga deullyeoyo.

시끄럽(시끄러우)+ㄴ 소리+가 들리+어요.
　　 시끄러운　　　　　　　　 들려요

시끄럽다 : loud
-ㄴ : An ending of a word that makes the preceding statement function as an adnominal phrase and refers to the present state.
소리 : sound; noise
가 : A postpositional particle referring to a subject under a certain state or situation, or the subject of an act.
들리다 : be heard; be audible

-어요 : (informal addressee-raising) A sentence-final ending used to describe a certain fact, ask a question, give an order, or advise.<description>

(74) 조용하다 [joyonghada]
quiet
No sound being heard

거리가 <u>조용해요</u>.
georiga joyonghaeyo.

거리+가 <u>조용하+여요</u>.
　　　　<u>조용해요</u>

거리 : street; road; avenue
가 : A postpositional particle referring to a subject under a certain state or situation, or the subject of an act.
조용하다 : quiet
-여요 : (informal addressee-raising) A sentence-final ending used to describe a certain fact, ask a question, give an order, or advise. <description>

(75) 지저분하다 [jijeobunhada]
messy
Disorderly and untidy.

길이 너무 <u>지저분해요</u>.
giri neomu jijeobunhaeyo.

길+이 너무 <u>지저분하+여요</u>.
　　　　　　<u>지저분해요</u>

길 : road; street; way
이 : A postpositional particle referring to a subject under a certain state or situation, or the agent of an action.
너무 : too
지저분하다 : messy

-여요 : (informal addressee-raising) A sentence-final ending used to describe a certain fact, ask a question, give an order, or advise. \<description\>

(76) 비싸다 [bissada]
expensive; costly
The price of an object or the cost to do something being higher than the average.

백화점은 시장보다 가격이 <u>비싸요</u>.
baekwajeomeun sijangboda gagyeogi bissayo.

백화점+은 시장+보다 가격+이 <u>비싸+아요</u>.
비싸요

백화점 : department store
은 : A postpositional particle used to indicate that a certain subject is the topic of a sentence.
시장 : market
보다 : A postpositional particle that indicates the subject of a comparison when comparing different things.
가격 : price
이 : A postpositional particle referring to a subject under a certain state or situation, or the agent of an action.
비싸다 : expensive; costly
-아요 : (informal addressee-raising) A sentence-final ending used to describe a certain fact, ask a question, give an order, or advise. \<description\>

(77) 싸다 [ssada]
cheap
Lower than usual in price.

이 동네는 집값이 <u>싸요</u>.
i dongneneun jipgapsi ssayo.

이 동네+는 집값+이 <u>싸+아요</u>.
싸요

이 : this

동네 : neighborhood

는 : A postpositional particle used to indicate that a certain subject is the topic of a sentence.

집값 : house price

이 : A postpositional particle referring to a subject under a certain state or situation, or the agent of an action.

싸다 : cheap

-아요 : (informal addressee-raising) A sentence-final ending used to describe a certain fact, ask a question, give an order, or advise. <description>

(78) 덥다 [deopda]

hot

For one's body to feel that the air is hot and the temperature high.

여름이 지났는데도 <u>더워요</u>.

yeoreumi jinanneundedo deowoyo.

여름+이 <u>지나+았+는데도</u> <u>덥(더우)+어요</u>.
　　　　　　지났는데도　　　　　더워요

여름 : summer

이 : A postpositional particle referring to a subject under a certain state or situation, or the agent of an action.

지나다 : pass; elapse

-았- : An ending of a word used to indicate that an event was completed in the past or its result continues in the present.

-는데도 : An expression used to indicate that the following situation will occur, regardless of the preceding situation.

덥다 : hot

-어요 : (informal addressee-raising) A sentence-final ending used to describe a certain fact, ask a question, give an order, or advise. <description>

(79) 따뜻하다 [ttatteutada]

warm

Being an appropriate, pleasant temperature, which is not too high.

날씨가 <u>따뜻해요</u>.

nalssiga ttatteutaeyo.

날씨+가 <u>따뜻하</u>+<u>여요</u>.
따뜻해요

날씨 : weather
가 : A postpositional particle referring to a subject under a certain state or situation, or the subject of an act.
따뜻하다 : warm
-여요 : (informal addressee-raising) A sentence-final ending used to describe a certain fact, ask a question, give an order, or advise. <description>

(80) 맑다 [makda]
clear; fine
(for the weather) Fine without clouds or mist.

가을 하늘은 푸르고 <u>맑아요</u>.
gaeul haneureun pureugo malgayo.

가을 하늘+은 푸르+고 맑+<u>아요</u>.

가을 : fall
하늘 : sky
은 : A postpositional particle used to indicate that a certain subject is the topic of a sentence.
푸르다 : blue; green
-고 : A connective ending used when listing more than two equal facts.
맑다 : clear; fine
-아요 : (informal addressee-raising) A sentence-final ending used to describe a certain fact, ask a question, give an order, or advise. <description>

(81) 선선하다 [seonseonhada]
cool; refreshing
Gentle and cool, when one feels a little cold.

이제 아침저녁으로 <u>선선해요</u>.
ije achimjeonyeogeuro seonseonhaeyo.

이제 아침저녁+으로 선선하+여요.
선선해요

이제 : now
아침저녁 : morning and evening; all day
으로 : A postpositional particle that indicates time.
선선하다 : cool; refreshing
-여요 : (informal addressee-raising) A sentence-final ending used to describe a certain fact, ask a question, give an order, or advise. <description>

(82) 쌀쌀하다 [ssalssalhada]

chilly; rather cold

The weather being cold to a degree that one feels a bit cold.

바람이 꽤 쌀쌀해요.
barami kkwae ssalssalhaeyo.

바람+이 꽤 쌀쌀하+여요.
쌀쌀해요

바람 : wind
이 : A postpositional particle referring to a subject under a certain state or situation, or the agent of an action.
꽤 : quite; fairly
쌀쌀하다 : chilly; rather cold
-여요 : (informal addressee-raising) A sentence-final ending used to describe a certain fact, ask a question, give an order, or advise. <description>

(83) 춥다 [chupda]

cold

(temperature) Low.

날이 추우니 따뜻하게 입으세요.
nari chuuni ttatteutage ibeuseyo.

날+이 춥(추우)+니 따뜻하+게 입+으세요.
　　　　추우니

날 : weather
이 : A postpositional particle referring to a subject under a certain state or situation, or the agent of an action.
춥다 : cold
-니 : A connective ending used when the preceding statement is the cause, reason, or premise for the following statement.
따뜻하다 : warm
-게 : A connective ending used when the preceding statement is the purpose, result, method, amount, etc., of something mentioned in the following statement.
입다 : wear; be dressed; put on
-으세요 : (informal addressee-raising) A sentence-final ending used to describe, ask a question, order, and request. <order>

(84) 흐리다 [heurida]
cloud; foggy
The weather not being clear due to clouds or fog.

안개 때문에 흐려서 앞이 안 보여요.
angae ttaemune heuryeoseo api an boyeoyo.

안개 때문+에 흐리+어서 앞+이 안 보이+어요.
　　　　　　흐려서　　　　　　보여요

안개 : fog; mist; haze
때문 : because; because of
에 : A postpositional particle to indicate that the preceding statement is the cause for something.
흐리다 : cloud; foggy
-어서 : A connective ending used for a reason or cause.
앞 : front
이 : A postpositional particle referring to a subject under a certain state or situation, or the agent of an action.
안 : not
보이다 : be viewed; be visible; be in sight
-어요 : (informal addressee-raising) A sentence-final ending used to describe a certain fact, ask a question, give an order, or advise. <description>

(85) 가늘다 [ganeulda]

thin

An object having a narrow width or being thin and long.

저는 손가락이 <u>가늘어요</u>.

jeoneun songaragi ganeureoyo.

저+는 손가락+이 가늘+어요.

저 : I; me
는 : A postpositional particle used to indicate that a certain subject is the topic of a sentence.
손가락 : finger
이 : A postpositional particle referring to a subject under a certain state or situation, or the agent of an action.
가늘다 : thin
-어요 : (informal addressee-raising) A sentence-final ending used to describe a certain fact, ask a question, give an order, or advise. <description>

(86) 같다 [gatda]

same; identical; equal

Not different from each other.

저는 여동생과 키가 <u>같아요</u>.

jeoneun yeodongsaenggwa kiga gatayo.

저+는 여동생+과 키+가 같+아요.

저 : I; me
는 : A postpositional particle used to indicate that a certain subject is the topic of a sentence.
여동생 : younger sister
과 : A postpositional word used to indicate the subject of comparison or the object that serves as a basis.
키 : height
가 : A postpositional particle referring to a subject under a certain state or situation, or the subject of an act.
같다 : same; identical; equal

-아요 : (informal addressee-raising) A sentence-final ending used to describe a certain fact, ask a question, give an order, or advise. \<description\>

(87) 굵다 [gukda]

thick

An object being long in circumference or wide in width.

저는 허리가 굵어요.

jeoneun heoriga gulgeoyo.

저+는 허리+가 굵+어요.

저 : I; me
는 : A postpositional particle used to indicate that a certain subject is the topic of a sentence.
허리 : waist
가 : A postpositional particle referring to a subject under a certain state or situation, or the subject of an act.
굵다 : thick
-어요 : (informal addressee-raising) A sentence-final ending used to describe a certain fact, ask a question, give an order, or advise. \<description\>

(88) 길다 [gilda]

long; lengthy; extensive

Two ends of an object being far apart.

치마 길이가 길어요.

chima giriga gireoyo.

치마 길이+가 길+어요.

치마 : skirt
길이 : length; distance
가 : A postpositional particle referring to a subject under a certain state or situation, or the subject of an act.
길다 : long; lengthy; extensive

-어요 : (informal addressee-raising) A sentence-final ending used to describe a certain fact, ask a question, give an order, or advise. <description>

(89) 깊다 [gipda]

deep

Having a very long distance from top to bottom or from outside to inside.

물이 깊<u>으니</u> 들어가지 마세요.

muri gipeuni deureogaji maseyo.

물+이 깊+<u>으니</u> <u>들어가</u>+[지 말(마)]+<u>세요</u>.
들어가지 마세요

물 : water

이 : A postpositional particle referring to a subject under a certain state or situation, or the agent of an action.

깊다 : deep

-으니 : A connective ending used when the preceding statement is the cause, reason, or premise for the following statement.

들어가다 : enter; go into

-지 말다 : An expression used to prohibit the act mentioned in the preceding statement.

-세요 : (informal addressee-raising) A sentence-final ending used to describe, ask a question, order, and request. <order>

(90) 낮다 [natda]

low

The length from top to bottom being short.

저는 굽이 낮은 구두를 즐겨 신어요.

jeoneun gubi najeun gudureul jeulgyeo sineoyo.

저+는 굽+이 낮+은 구두+를 <u>즐기</u>+어 신+어요.
즐겨

저 : I; me

는 : A postpositional particle used to indicate that a certain subject is the topic of a sentence.

굽 : heel

이 : A postpositional particle referring to a subject under a certain state or situation, or the agent of an action.

낮다 : low

-은 : An ending of a word that makes the preceding word function as an adnominal phrase and refers to the present state.

구두 : shoes

를 : A postpositional particle used to indicate the subject that an act has a direct influence on.

즐기다 : enjoy; appreciate; take pleasure in

-어 : A connective ending used when the preceding statement happened before the following statement or was the ways or means to the following statement.

신다 : put on; wear

-어요 : (informal addressee-raising) A sentence-final ending used to describe a certain fact, ask a question, give an order, or advise. <description>

(91) 넓다 [neolda]

broad

The size of the surface, floor, etc., being large.

넓은 이마를 가리려고 앞머리를 내렸어요.

neolbeun imareul gariryeogo ammeorireul naeryeosseoyo.

넓+은 이마+를 가리+려고 앞머리+를 내리+었+어요.
내렸어요

넓다 : broad

-은 : An ending of a word that makes the preceding word function as an adnominal phrase and refers to the present state.

이마 : forehead

를 : A postpositional particle used to indicate the subject that an act has a direct influence on.

가리다 : block; screen; shield; obscure

-려고 : A connective ending used to indicate that one has an intention or desire of doing a certain act.

앞머리 : forelock

를 : A postpositional particle used to indicate the subject that an act has a direct influence on.

내리다 : pull down; hang

-었- : An ending of a word used to indicate that an event was completed in the past or its result continues in the present.

-어요 : (informal addressee-raising) A sentence-final ending used to describe a certain fact, ask a question, give an order, or advise. <description>

(92) 높다 [nopda]

high; lofty

The length from bottom to top being long.

서울에는 높은 빌딩이 많아요.

seoureneun nopeun bildingi manayo.

서울+에+는 높+은 빌딩+이 많+아요.

서울 : Seoul

에 : A postpositional particle to indicate that the preceding statement refers to a certain place or space.

는 : A postpositional particle used to indicate that a certain subject is the topic of a sentence.

높다 : high; lofty

-은 : An ending of a word that makes the preceding word function as an adnominal phrase and refers to the present state.

빌딩 : building

이 : A postpositional particle referring to a subject under a certain state or situation, or the agent of an action.

많다 : plentiful; many; a lot of

-아요 : (informal addressee-raising) A sentence-final ending used to describe a certain fact, ask a question, give an order, or advise. <description>

(93) 다르다 [dareuda]

different; other

Not the same as each other.

저는 언니와 성격이 많이 달라요.

jeoneun eonniwa seonggyeogi mani dallayo.

저+는 언니+와 성격+이 많이 다르(달르)+아요.

달라요

저 : I; me

는 : A postpositional particle used to indicate that a certain subject is the topic of a sentence.

언니 : older sister

와 : A postpositional particle used to indicate that something is the subject of a comparison or subject of a standard.

성격 : personality; character

이 : A postpositional particle referring to a subject under a certain state or situation, or the agent of an action.

많이 : much; in large numbers; in large amounts

다르다 : different; other

-아요 : (informal addressee-raising) A sentence-final ending used to describe a certain fact, ask a question, give an order, or advise. <description>

(94) 닮다 [damda]

resemble

For two or more people or objects to have similar appearances or qualities.

저는 언니와 안 닮았어요.

jeoneun eonniwa an dalmasseoyo.

저+는 언니+와 안 닮+았+어요.

저 : I; me

는 : A postpositional particle used to indicate that a certain subject is the topic of a sentence.

언니 : older sister

와 : A postpositional particle used to indicate that something is the subject of a comparison or subject of a standard.

안 : not

닮다 : resemble

-았- : An ending of a word used to indicate that an event was completed in the past or its result continues in the present.

-어요 : (informal addressee-raising) A sentence-final ending used to describe a certain fact, ask a question, give an order, or advise. <description>

(95) 두껍다 [dukkeopda]

thick

The measured distance between one side of an object and the other side being long.

고기를 두껍게 썰어서 잘 안 익어요.

gogireul dukkeopge sseoreoseo jal an igeoyo.

고기+를 두껍+게 썰+어서 잘 안 익+어요.

고기 : meat
를 : A postpositional particle used to indicate the subject that an act has a direct influence on.
두껍다 : thick
-게 : A connective ending used when the preceding statement is the purpose, result, method, amount, etc., of something mentioned in the following statement.
썰다 : slice; cut
-어서 : A connective ending used for a reason or cause.
잘 : well
안 : not
익다 : be cooked
-어요 : (informal addressee-raising) A sentence-final ending used to describe a certain fact, ask a question, give an order, or advise. <description>

(96) 똑같다 [ttokgatda]

exactly the same; equivalent to

Not a bit different from each other in shape, amount, quality, etc.

저와 똑같은 이름을 가진 사람들이 많아요.
jeowa ttokgateun ireumeul gajin saramdeuri manayo.

저+와 똑같+은 이름+을 가지+ㄴ 사람+들+이 많+아요.
　　　　　　　　　　　　가진

저 : I; me
와 : A postpositional particle used to indicate that something is the subject of a comparison or subject of a standard.
똑같다 : exactly the same; equivalent to
-은 : An ending of a word that makes the preceding word function as an adnominal phrase and refers to the present state.
이름 : name; given name
을 : A postpositional particle used to indicate the subject that an action has a direct influence on.
가지다 : have; hold
-ㄴ : An ending of a word that makes the preceding statement function as an adnominal phrase and indicates that an event or action has been completed and its state continues.
사람 : human; man
들 : A suffix used to mean plural.

이 : A postpositional particle referring to a subject under a certain state or situation, or the agent of an action.

많다 : plentiful; many; a lot of

-아요 : (informal addressee-raising) A sentence-final ending used to describe a certain fact, ask a question, give an order, or advise. <description>

(97) 멋있다 [meoditda]

nice; stylish; elegant

Very good or great.

새로 산 옷인데 멋있어요?

saero san osinde meosisseoyo?

새로 <u>사+ㄴ</u> 옷+이+ㄴ데 멋있+어요?
　　　산　　옷인데

새로 : freshly

사다 : buy; purchase; get

-ㄴ : An ending of a word that makes the preceding statement function as an adnominal phrase and indicates that an event or action has been completed and its state continues.

옷 : clothes; garment

이다 : A predicate particle indicating the meaning of the attribute or category of the thing that the subject of the sentence refers to.

-ㄴ데 : A connective ending used to talk in advance about a situation to follow.

멋있다 : nice; stylish; elegant

-어요 : (informal addressee-raising) A sentence-final ending used to describe a certain fact, ask a question, give an order, or advise. <question>

(98) 비슷하다 [biseutada]

similar

Two or more sizes, shapes, states, qualities, etc., being not the same, but being alike in many ways.

학교 건물이 모두 비슷해요.

hakgyo geonmuri modu biseutaeyo.

학교 건물+이 모두 <u>비슷하+여요</u>.
　　　　　　　　비슷해요

학교 : school

건물 : building; structure; edifice

이 : A postpositional particle referring to a subject under a certain state or situation, or the agent of an action.

모두 : all of

비슷하다 : similar

-여요 : (informal addressee-raising) A sentence-final ending used to describe a certain fact, ask a question, give an order, or advise. <description>

(99) 얇다 [yalda]

thin

Not thick.

얇은 옷을 입고 나와서 좀 추워요.

yalbeun oseul ipgo nawaseo jom chuwoyo.

얇+은 옷+을 입+고 나오+아서 좀 춥(추우)+어요.
　　　　　　　　　　　나와서　　　　　추워요

얇다 : thin

-은 : An ending of a word that makes the preceding word function as an adnominal phrase and refers to the present state.

옷 : clothes; garment

을 : A postpositional particle used to indicate the subject that an action has a direct influence on.

입다 : wear; be dressed; put on

-고 : A connective ending used when an action or result of the preceding statement remains the same while the following action happens.

나오다 : come out; get out

-아서 : A connective ending used for a reason or cause.

좀 : a little

춥다 : cold; chilly

-어요 : (informal addressee-raising) A sentence-final ending used to describe a certain fact, ask a question, give an order, or advise. <description>

(100) 작다 [jakda]

small; little

Lower than others or average in length, area, volume, etc.

언니는 키가 저보다 <u>작아요</u>.

eonnineun kiga jeoboda jagayo.

언니+는 키+가 저+보다 작+아요.

언니 : older sister
는 : A postpositional particle used to indicate that a certain subject is the topic of a sentence.
키 : height
가 : A postpositional particle referring to a subject under a certain state or situation, or the subject of an act.
저 : I; me
보다 : A postpositional particle that indicates the subject of a comparison when comparing different things.
작다 : small; little
-아요 : (informal addressee-raising) A sentence-final ending used to describe a certain fact, ask a question, give an order, or advise. <description>

(101) 좁다 [jopda]

small

A surface, floor, etc., being small in size.

여기는 주차장이 <u>좁아요</u>.

yeogineun juchajangi jobayo.

여기+는 주차장+이 좁+아요.

여기 : here; this
는 : A postpositional particle used to indicate that a certain subject is the topic of a sentence.
주차장 : parking lot
이 : A postpositional particle referring to a subject under a certain state or situation, or the agent of an action.
좁다 : small
-아요 : (informal addressee-raising) A sentence-final ending used to describe a certain fact, ask a question, give an order, or advise. <description>

(102) 짧다 [jjalda]

short

The distance between the two ends of a space or object being close.

긴 머리를 <u>짧게</u> 잘랐어요.

gin meorireul jjalge jallasseoyo.

<u>길(기)+ㄴ</u> 머리+를 짧+게 <u>자르(잘ㄹ)+았</u>+어요.
   긴   잘랐어요

길다 : long; lengthy; extensive

-ㄴ : An ending of a word that makes the preceding statement function as an adnominal phrase and refers to the present state.

머리 : hair

를 : A postpositional particle used to indicate the subject that an act has a direct influence on.

짧다 : short

-게 : A connective ending used when the preceding statement is the purpose, result, method, amount, etc., of something mentioned in the following statement.

자르다 : cut; sever; chop

-았- : An ending of a word used to indicate that an event was completed in the past or its result continues in the present.

-어요 : (informal addressee-raising) A sentence-final ending used to describe a certain fact, ask a question, give an order, or advise. <description>

(103) 크다 [keuda]

big; large

A length, width, height, volume, etc., exceeding an ordinary degree.

피자가 생각보다 훨씬 <u>커요</u>.

pijaga saenggakboda hwolssin keoyo.

피자+가 생각+보다 훨씬 <u>크(ㅋ)+어요</u>.
                              커요

피자 : pizza

가 : A postpositional particle referring to a subject under a certain state or situation, or the subject of an act.

생각 : thought; expectation; imagination

보다 : A postpositional particle that indicates the subject of a comparison when comparing different things.

훨씬 : by far; much; a lot

크다 : big; large

-어요 : (informal addressee-raising) A sentence-final ending used to describe a certain fact, ask a question, give an order, or advise. <description>

(104) 화려하다 [hwaryeohada]
colorful; flashy; splendid

Looking good, being beautiful, bright, and shiny.

방 안을 화려하게 꾸몄어요.

bang aneul hwaryeohage kkumyeosseoyo.

방 안+을 화려하+게 꾸미+었+어요.
꾸몄어요

방 : room

안 : inside

을 : A postpositional particle used to indicate the subject that an action has a direct influence on.

화려하다 : colorful; flashy; splendid

-게 : A connective ending used when the preceding statement is the purpose, result, method, amount, etc., of something mentioned in the following statement.

꾸미다 : decorate; adorn

-었- : An ending of a word used to indicate that an event was completed in the past or its result continues in the present.

-어요 : (informal addressee-raising) A sentence-final ending used to describe a certain fact, ask a question, give an order, or advise. <description>

(105) 가볍다 [gabyeopda]
light

Weighing little.

이 노트북은 아주 가벼워요.

i noteubugeun aju gabyeowoyo.

이 노트북+은 아주 <u>가볍(가벼우)</u>+어요.
가벼워요

이 : this
노트북 : laptop; notebook computer
은 : A postpositional particle used to indicate that a certain subject is the topic of a sentence.
아주 : very; so; extremely
가볍다 : light
-어요 : (informal addressee-raising) A sentence-final ending used to describe a certain fact, ask a question, give an order, or advise. <description>

(106) 강하다 [ganghada]

strong; powerful
Having strength.

오늘은 바람이 <u>강하게</u> 불고 있어요.
oneureun barami ganghage bulgo isseoyo.

오늘+은 바람+이 강하+게 불+[고 있]+어요.

오늘 : today
은 : A postpositional particle used to indicate that a certain subject is the topic of a sentence.
바람 : wind
이 : A postpositional particle referring to a subject under a certain state or situation, or the agent of an action.
강하다 : strong; powerful
-게 : A connective ending used when the preceding statement is the purpose, result, method, amount, etc., of something mentioned in the following statement.
불다 : blow
-고 있다 : An expression used to state that the act mentioned in the preceding statement is continued.
-어요 : (informal addressee-raising) A sentence-final ending used to describe a certain fact, ask a question, give an order, or advise. <description>

(107) 무겁다 [mugeopda]

heavy; weighty
Weighing a lot.

저는 보기보다 <u>무거워요</u>.

jeoneun bogiboda mugeowoyo.

저+는 보+기+보다 <u>무겁(무거우)+어요</u>.
무거워요

저 : I; me

는 : A postpositional particle used to indicate that a certain subject is the topic of a sentence.

보다 : see; look at; notice

-기 : An ending of a word used to make the preceding word function as a noun.

보다 : A postpositional particle that indicates the subject of a comparison when comparing different things.

무겁다 : heavy; weighty

-어요 : (informal addressee-raising) A sentence-final ending used to describe a certain fact, ask a question, give an order, or advise. <description>

(108) 부드럽다 [budeureopda]

soft; smooth

Silky, not rough or stiff, to the touch.

이 운동화는 가볍고 안쪽이 <u>부드러워요</u>.

i undonghwaneun gabyeopgo anjjogi budeureowoyo.

이 운동화+는 가볍+고 안쪽+이 <u>부드럽(부드러우)+어요</u>.
부드러워요

이 : this

운동화 : running shoes; sneakers

는 : A postpositional particle used to indicate that a certain subject is the topic of a sentence.

가볍다 : light

-고 : A connective ending used when listing more than two equal facts.

안쪽 : the inside; the interior; inner part

이 : A postpositional particle referring to a subject under a certain state or situation, or the agent of an action.

부드럽다 : soft; smooth

-어요 : (informal addressee-raising) A sentence-final ending used to describe a certain fact, ask a question, give an order, or advise. <description>

(109) 새롭다 [saeropda]

new; fresh

Being different from existing ones or never having existed.

요즘 <u>새로운</u> 취미가 생겼어요?

yojeum saeroun chwimiga saenggyeosseoyo?

요즘 <u>새롭(새로우)+ㄴ</u> 취미+가 <u>생기+었+어요</u>?
　　　새로운　　　　　　　생겼어요

요즘 : nowadays; these days
새롭다 : new; fresh
-ㄴ : An ending of a word that makes the preceding statement function as an adnominal phrase and refers to the present state.
취미 : hobby
가 : A postpositional particle referring to a subject under a certain state or situation, or the subject of an act.
생기다 : be formed; come into being
-었- : An ending of a word used to indicate that an event was completed in the past or its result continues in the present.
-어요 : (informal addressee-raising) A sentence-final ending used to describe a certain fact, ask a question, give an order, or advise. <question>

(110) 느리다 [neurida]

slow; sluggish

Taking a long time to do something.

저는 걸음이 <u>느려요</u>.

jeoneun georeumi neuryeoyo.

저+는 걸음+이 <u>느리+어요</u>.
　　　　　　느려요

저 : I; me
는 : A postpositional particle used to indicate that a certain subject is the topic of a sentence.
걸음 : step; walk

이 : A postpositional particle referring to a subject under a certain state or situation, or the agent of an action.

느리다 : slow; sluggish

-어요 : (informal addressee-raising) A sentence-final ending used to describe a certain fact, ask a question, give an order, or advise. <description>

(111) 빠르다 [ppareuda]

fast; quick

Taking a short time to accomplish certain actions.

제 친구는 말이 너무 <u>빨라요</u>.

je chinguneun mari neomu ppallayo.

저+<u>의</u> 친구+는 말+이 너무 <u>빠르(빨ㄹ)+아요</u>.
　제　　　　　　　　　　　　　　<u>빨라요</u>

저 : I; me

의 : A postpositional particle used to indicate that the referent of the following word is owned by, belongs to, is related to, originates from, or is the object of what the preceding word indicates.

친구 : friend

는 : A postpositional particle used to indicate that a certain subject is the topic of a sentence.

말 : speech; words

이 : A postpositional particle referring to a subject under a certain state or situation, or the agent of an action.

너무 : too

빠르다 : fast; quick

-아요 : (informal addressee-raising) A sentence-final ending used to describe a certain fact, ask a question, give an order, or advise. <description>

(112) 뜨겁다 [tteugeopda]

hot

(temperature) High.

국물이 <u>뜨거우니</u> 조심하세요.

gungmuri tteugeouni josimhaseyo.

국물+이 <u>뜨겁(뜨거우)+니</u> 조심하+세요.
　　　　뜨거우니

국물 : broth, stock, or soup
이 : A postpositional particle referring to a subject under a certain state or situation, or the agent of an action.
뜨겁다 : hot
-니 : A connective ending used when the preceding statement is the cause, reason, or premise for the following statement.
조심하다 : practice caution
-세요 : (informal addressee-raising) A sentence-final ending used to describe, ask a question, order, and request. <order>

(113) 차갑다 [chagapda]
cold
The touch of something on one's skin being cold.

이 물은 <u>차갑지</u> 않아요.
i mureun chagapji anayo.

이 물+은 차갑+[지 않]+아요.

이 : this
물 : water
은 : A postpositional particle used to indicate that a certain subject is the topic of a sentence.
차갑다 : cold
-지 않다 : An expression used to deny the act or state indicated in the preceding statement.
-아요 : (informal addressee-raising) A sentence-final ending used to describe a certain fact, ask a question, give an order, or advise. <description>

(114) 차다 [chada]
cold
Lacking warmth due to low temperature.

저는 손이 찬 편이에요.
jeoneun soni chan pyeonieyo.

저+는 손+이 차+[ㄴ 편이]+에요.
찬 편이에요

저 : I; me
는 : A postpositional particle used to indicate that a certain subject is the topic of a sentence.
손 : hand
이 : A postpositional particle referring to a subject under a certain state or situation, or the agent of an action.
차다 : cold
-ㄴ 편이다 : An expression used to indicate that something has a certain tendency or is classified as such, instead of being sure of it.
-에요 : (informal addressee-raising) A sentence-final ending used when describing a certain fact or asking a question. <description>

(115) 밝다 [bakda]

light; brilliant; luminous
The light emanating from something being bright.

조명이 너무 밝아서 눈이 부셔요.
jomyeongi neomu balgaseo nuni busyeoyo.

조명+이 너무 밝+아서 눈+이 부시+어요.
부셔요

조명 : lighting
이 : A postpositional particle referring to a subject under a certain state or situation, or the agent of an action.
너무 : too
밝다 : light; brilliant; luminous
-아서 : A connective ending used for a reason or cause.
눈 : eye
이 : A postpositional particle referring to a subject under a certain state or situation, or the agent of an action.
부시다 : dazzling
-어요 : (informal addressee-raising) A sentence-final ending used to describe a certain fact, ask a question, give an order, or advise. <description>

(116) 어둡다 [eodupda]

dark; dim

Not bright due to the lack of light.

해가 져서 밖이 <u>어두워요</u>.

haega jeoseo bakki eoduwoyo.

해+가 <u>지+어서</u> 밖+이 <u>어둡(어두우)+어요</u>.
　　　　져서　　　　　　　어두워요

해 : sun

가 : A postpositional particle referring to a subject under a certain state or situation, or the subject of an act.

지다 : set

-어서 : A connective ending used for a reason or cause.

밖 : being outside; being outdoors

이 : A postpositional particle referring to a subject under a certain state or situation, or the agent of an action.

어둡다 : dark; dim

-어요 : (informal addressee-raising) A sentence-final ending used to describe a certain fact, ask a question, give an order, or advise. <description>

(117) 까맣다 [kkamata]

pitch-dark

Deep-black like the night sky devoid of light.

머리를 <u>까맣게</u> 염색했어요.

meorireul kkamake yeomsaekaesseoyo.

머리+를 까맣+게 <u>염색하+였+어요</u>.
　　　　　　　　　염색했어요

머리 : hair

를 : A postpositional particle used to indicate the subject that an act has a direct influence on.

까맣다 : pitch-dark

-게 : A connective ending used when the preceding statement is the purpose, result, method, amount, etc., of something mentioned in the following statement.

염색하다 : dye

-였- : An ending of a word used to indicate that an event was completed in the past or its result continues in the present.

-어요 : (informal addressee-raising) A sentence-final ending used to describe a certain fact, ask a question, give an order, or advise. <description>

(118) 검다 [geomda]

black; dark

Dark black like a night sky with no light.

햇볕에 살이 <u>검게</u> 탔어요.

haetbyeote sari geomge tasseoyo.

햇볕+에 살+이 검+게 <u>타+았+어요</u>.
탔어요

햇볕 : sunshine; sunlight

에 : A postpositional particle to indicate that the preceding statement is the cause for something.

살 : flesh; weight

이 : A postpositional particle referring to a subject under a certain state or situation, or the agent of an action.

검다 : black; dark

-게 : A connective ending used when the preceding statement is the purpose, result, method, amount, etc., of something mentioned in the following statement.

타다 : be tanned

-았- : An ending of a word used to indicate that an event was completed in the past or its result continues in the present.

-어요 : (informal addressee-raising) A sentence-final ending used to describe a certain fact, ask a question, give an order, or advise. <description>

(119) 노랗다 [norata]

yellow

Having color like that of a banana or lemon.

저 사람은 머리 색깔이 <u>노래요</u>.

jeo sarameun meori saekkkari noraeyo.

저 사람+은 머리 색깔+이 <u>노랗+아요</u>.

노래요

저 : that
사람 : human; man
은 : A postpositional particle used to indicate that a certain subject is the topic of a sentence.
머리 : hair
색깔 : color; hue; tint
이 : A postpositional particle referring to a subject under a certain state or situation, or the agent of an action.
노랗다 : yellow
-아요 : (informal addressee-raising) A sentence-final ending used to describe a certain fact, ask a question, give an order, or advise. <description>

(120) 붉다 [bukda]

red

The color of something being like that of blood or a ripe chili pepper.

<u>붉은</u> 태양이 떠오르고 있어요.

bulgeun taeyangi tteooreugo isseoyo.

붉+은 태양+이 떠오르+[고 있]+어요.

붉다 : red
-은 : An ending of a word that makes the preceding word function as an adnominal phrase and refers to the present state.
태양 : sun
이 : A postpositional particle referring to a subject under a certain state or situation, or the agent of an action.
떠오르다 : rise; come up
-고 있다 : An expression used to state that the act mentioned in the preceding statement is continued.
-어요 : (informal addressee-raising) A sentence-final ending used to describe a certain fact, ask a question, give an order, or advise. <description>

(121) 빨갛다 [ppalgata]

crimson

Brightly deep red like the color of blood or a ripe chili pepper.

코가 왜 이렇게 <u>빨개요</u>?

koga wae ireoke ppalgaeyo?

코+가 왜 이렇+게 <u>빨갛+아요</u>?
빨개요

코 : nose
가 : A postpositional particle referring to a subject under a certain state or situation, or the subject of an act.
왜 : why
이렇다 : so; like this
-게 : A connective ending used when the preceding statement is the purpose, result, method, amount, etc., of something mentioned in the following statement.
빨갛다 : crimson
-아요 : (informal addressee-raising) A sentence-final ending used to describe a certain fact, ask a question, give an order, or advise. <question>

(122) 파랗다 [parata]

blue

A color being brightly and vividly blue like that of a clear fall sky or deep sea.

왜 이마에 멍이 <u>파랗게</u> 들었어요?

wae imae meongi parake deureosseoyo?

왜 이마+에 멍+이 파랗+게 들+었+어요?

왜 : why
이마 : forehead
에 : A postpositional particle to indicate that the preceding statement refers to a certain place or space.
멍 : bruise; black and blue
이 : A postpositional particle referring to a subject under a certain state or situation, or the agent of an action.
파랗다 : blue
-게 : A connective ending used when the preceding statement is the purpose, result, method, amount, etc., of something mentioned in the following statement.
들다 : get; have; catch; develop
-었- : An ending of a word used to indicate that an event was completed in the past or its result continues in the present.

-어요 : (informal addressee-raising) A sentence-final ending used to describe a certain fact, ask a question, give an order, or advise. <question>

(123) 푸르다 [pureuda]
blue; green
Clear and vivid blue, like that of a clear fall sky, deep ocean, or fresh grass.

바다가 넓고 <u>푸르러요</u>.

badaga neolgo pureureoyo.

바다+가 넓+고 <u>푸르+어요(러요)</u>.
　　　　　　　　푸르러요

바다 : sea
가 : A postpositional particle referring to a subject under a certain state or situation, or the subject of an act.
넓다 : broad
-고 : A connective ending used when listing more than two equal facts.
푸르다 : blue; green
-어요 : (informal addressee-raising) A sentence-final ending used to describe a certain fact, ask a question, give an order, or advise. <description>

(124) 하얗다 [hayata]
white
Clearly bright, white like the color of snow or milk.

눈이 내려서 세상이 <u>하얗게</u> 변했어요.

nuni naeryeoseo sesangi hayake byeonhaesseoyo.

눈+이 <u>내리+어서</u> 세상+이 하얗+게 <u>변하+였+어요</u>.
　　　내려서　　　　　　　　변했어요

눈 : snow
이 : A postpositional particle referring to a subject under a certain state or situation, or the agent of an action.
내리다 : fall; descend

-어서 : A connective ending used for a reason or cause.

세상 : world

이 : A postpositional particle referring to a subject under a certain state or situation, or the agent of an action.

하얗다 : white

-게 : A connective ending used when the preceding statement is the purpose, result, method, amount, etc., of something mentioned in the following statement.

변하다 : change; turn; become different

-였- : An ending of a word used to indicate that an event was completed in the past or its result continues in the present.

-어요 : (informal addressee-raising) A sentence-final ending used to describe a certain fact, ask a question, give an order, or advise. <description>

(125) 희다 [hida]

white

Bright and clear like the color of snow or milk.

동생은 얼굴이 <u>희고</u> 머리카락이 까매요.

dongsaengeun eolguri huigo meorikaragi kkamaeyo.

동생+은 얼굴+이 희+고 머리카락+이 <u>까맣+아요</u>.
까매요

동생 : brother; sister

은 : A postpositional particle used to indicate that a certain subject is the topic of a sentence.

얼굴 : face

이 : A postpositional particle referring to a subject under a certain state or situation, or the agent of an action.

희다 : white

-고 : A connective ending used when listing more than two equal facts.

머리카락 : hair

이 : A postpositional particle referring to a subject under a certain state or situation, or the agent of an action.

까맣다 : pitch-dark

-아요 : (informal addressee-raising) A sentence-final ending used to describe a certain fact, ask a question, give an order, or advise. <description>

(126) 많다 [manta]

plentiful; many; a lot of

A number, amount, etc., exceeding a certain standard.

저는 호기심이 <u>많아요</u>.

jeoneun hogisimi manayo.

저+는 호기심+이 많+아요.

저 : I; me
는 : A postpositional particle used to indicate that a certain subject is the topic of a sentence.
호기심 : curiosity; inquisitiveness
이 : A postpositional particle referring to a subject under a certain state or situation, or the agent of an action.
많다 : plentiful; many; a lot of
-아요 : (informal addressee-raising) A sentence-final ending used to describe a certain fact, ask a question, give an order, or advise. <description>

(127) 부족하다 [bujokada]

insufficient

Not enough or less than what is needed.

사업을 하기에 돈이 많이 <u>부족해요</u>.

saeobeul hagie doni mani bujokaeyo.

사업+을 하+기+에 돈+이 많이 <u>부족하+여요</u>.
                         부족해요

사업 : business
을 : A postpositional particle used to indicate the subject that an action has a direct influence on.
하다 : do; perform
-기 : An ending of a word used to make the preceding word function as a noun.
에 : A postpositional particle to indicate that the preceding statement is the condition, environment, state, etc., of something.
돈 : money
이 : A postpositional particle referring to a subject under a certain state or situation, or the agent of an action.

많이 : much; in large numbers; in large amounts

부족하다 : insufficient

-여요 : (informal addressee-raising) A sentence-final ending used to describe a certain fact, ask a question, give an order, or advise. <description>

(128) 적다 [jeokda]

little; a little

Not meeting a certain standard in terms of number, quantity or degree.

배고픈데 음식 양이 너무 <u>적어요</u>.

baegopeunde eumsik yangi neomu jeogeoyo.

<u>배고프</u>+ㄴ데 음식 양+이 너무 적+어요.
 배고픈데

배고프다 : hungry

-ㄴ데 : A connective ending used to talk in advance about a situation to follow.

음식 : food

양 : quantity; amount

이 : A postpositional particle referring to a subject under a certain state or situation, or the agent of an action.

너무 : too

적다 : little; a little

-어요 : (informal addressee-raising) A sentence-final ending used to describe a certain fact, ask a question, give an order, or advise. <description>

(129) 낫다 [natda]

better

Something being better than another thing.

몸이 아플 때에는 쉬는 것이 제일 <u>나아요</u>.

momi apeul ttaeeneun swineun geosi jeil naayo.

몸+이 <u>아프</u>+[ㄹ 때]+에+는 쉬+[는 것]+이 제일 <u>낫(나)</u>+아요.
 아플 때에는   나아요

몸 : body

이 : A postpositional particle referring to a subject under a certain state or situation, or the agent of an action.

아프다 : hurting; aching

-ㄹ 때 : An expression used to indicate the duration, period, or occasion of a certain act or situation.

에 : A postpositional particle to indicate that the preceding statement refers to the time.

는 : A postpositional particle used to indicate that a certain subject is the topic of a sentence.

쉬다 : rest; repose; take a rest

-는 것 : An expression used to enable a non-noun word to be used as a noun in a sentence or to be used in front of '이다' (be).

이 : A postpositional particle referring to a subject under a certain state or situation, or the agent of an action.

제일 : most

낫다 : better

-아요 : (informal addressee-raising) A sentence-final ending used to describe a certain fact, ask a question, give an order, or advise. <description>

(130) 분명하다 [bunmyeonghada]

distinct

A shape or sound being clear, not vague.

크고 <u>분명한</u> 목소리로 말해 주세요.

keugo bunmyeonghan moksoriro malhae juseyo.

크+고 <u>분명하+ㄴ</u> 목소리+로 말하+[여 주]+세요.
　　　　<u>분명한</u>　　　　　　　　말해 주세요

크다 : loud

-고 : A connective ending used when listing more than two equal facts.

분명하다 : distinct

-ㄴ : An ending of a word that makes the preceding statement function as an adnominal phrase and refers to the present state.

목소리 : voice

로 : A postpositional particle that indicates a method or way to do something.

말하다 : say; tell; speak; talk

-여 주다 : An expression used to indicate that one does the act mentioned in the preceding statement for someone.

-세요 : (informal addressee-raising) A sentence-final ending used to describe, ask a question, order, and request. <request>

(131) 심하다 [simhada]

severe; harsh

The degree of something being excessive.

감기에 <u>심하게</u> 걸렸어요.

gamgie simhage geollyeosseoyo.

감기+에 심하+게 <u>걸리+었+어요</u>.
걸렸어요

감기 : cold

에 : A postpositional particle to indicate that the preceding statement is the subject that is influenced by a certain action, emotion, etc.

심하다 : severe; harsh

-게 : A connective ending used when the preceding statement is the purpose, result, method, amount, etc., of something mentioned in the following statement.

걸리다 : catch; contract

-었- : An ending of a word used to indicate that an event was completed in the past or its result continues in the present.

-어요 : (informal addressee-raising) A sentence-final ending used to describe a certain fact, ask a question, give an order, or advise. <description>

(132) 알맞다 [almatda]

appropriate; proper; suitable

Satisfying a certain standard, condition, or degree without being excessive or insufficient.

물 온도가 목욕하기에 딱 <u>알맞아요</u>.

mul ondoga mogyokagie ttak almajayo.

물 온도+가 목욕하+기+에 딱 알맞+아요.

물 : water

온도 : temperature

가 : A postpositional particle referring to a subject under a certain state or situation, or the subject of an act.

목욕하다 : take a bath; bathe

-기 : An ending of a word used to make the preceding word function as a noun.

에 : A postpositional particle to indicate that the preceding statement is the condition, environment,
딱 : precisely
알맞다 : appropriate; proper; suitable
-아요 : (informal addressee-raising) A sentence-final ending used to describe a certain fact, ask a question, give an order, or advise. <description>

(133) 적당하다 [jeokdanghada]
adequate

Meeting requirements or conditions, or being appropriate in terms of degree.

하루 수면 시간은 일곱 시간 정도가 <u>적당해요</u>.
haru sumyeon siganeun ilgop sigan jeongdoga jeokdanghaeyo.

하루 수면 시간+은 일곱 시간 정도+가 <u>적당하</u>+여요.
적당해요

하루 : day
수면 : sleep
시간 : time
은 : A postpositional particle used to indicate that a certain subject is the topic of a sentence.
일곱 : seven
시간 : hour
정도 : being approximate
가 : A postpositional particle referring to a subject under a certain state or situation, or the subject of an act.
적당하다 : adequate
-여요 : (informal addressee-raising) A sentence-final ending used to describe a certain fact, ask a question, give an order, or advise. <description>

(134) 정확하다 [jeonghwakada]
accurate

Right and certain

<u>정확한</u> 한국어 발음을 하고 싶어요.
jeonghwakan hangugeo bareumeul hago sipeoyo.

<u>정확하</u>+ㄴ 한국어 발음+을 하+[고 싶]+어요.
   정확한

정확하다 : accurate

-ㄴ : An ending of a word that makes the preceding statement function as an adnominal phrase and refers to the present state.

한국어 : Korean; Korean language

발음 : pronunciation

을 : A postpositional particle used to indicate the subject that an action has a direct influence on.

하다 : do; perform

-고 싶다 : An expression used to state that the speaker wants to do the act mentioned in the preceding statement.

-어요 : (informal addressee-raising) A sentence-final ending used to describe a certain fact, ask a question, give an order, or advise. <description>

(135) 중요하다 [jungyohada]

important

Valuable and indispensable.

살을 뺄 때는 운동이 <u>중요해요</u>.

sareul ppael ttaeneun undongi jungyohaeyo.

살+을 <u>빼</u>+[ㄹ 때]+는 운동+이 <u>중요하</u>+여요.
        뺄 때는   중요해요

살 : flesh; weight

을 : A postpositional particle used to indicate the subject that an action has a direct influence on.

빼다 : lose; remove

-ㄹ 때 : An expression used to indicate the duration, period, or occasion of a certain act or situation.

는 : A postpositional particle used to indicate that a certain subject is the topic of a sentence.

운동 : exercise

이 : A postpositional particle referring to a subject under a certain state or situation, or the agent of an action.

중요하다 : important

-여요 : (informal addressee-raising) A sentence-final ending used to describe a certain fact, ask a question, give an order, or advise. <description>

(136) 진하다 [jinhada]

thick; strong

The concentration of a liquid being high.

커피가 너무 <u>진해요</u>.

keopiga neomu jinhaeyo.

커피+가 너무 <u>진하+여요</u>.
진해요

커피 : coffee

가 : A postpositional particle referring to a subject under a certain state or situation, or the subject of an act.

너무 : too

진하다 : thick; strong

-여요 : (informal addressee-raising) A sentence-final ending used to describe a certain fact, ask a question, give an order, or advise. <description>

(137) 충분하다 [chungbunhada]

sufficient; enough

Being ample, without shortage.

저는 이 빵 하나면 <u>충분해요</u>.

jeoneun i ppang hanamyeon chungbunhaeyo.

저+는 이 빵 <u>하나+이+면</u> <u>충분하+여요</u>.
하나면   충분해요

저 : I; me

는 : A postpositional particle used to indicate that a certain subject is the topic of a sentence.

이 : this

빵 : bread

하나 : one

이다 : A predicate particle indicating the meaning of the attribute or category of the thing that the subject of the sentence refers to.

-면 : A connective ending used when the preceding statement becomes the reason or condition of the following statement.

충분하다 : sufficient; enough

-여요 : (informal addressee-raising) A sentence-final ending used to describe a certain fact, ask a question, give an order, or advise. <description>

필수(essentials)

문법(grammar)

1. 모음 : 사람이 목청을 울려 내는 소리로, 공기의 흐름이 방해를 받지 않고 나는 소리.

vowel

A sound made by vibrating one's vocal cords without obstructing the flow of air.

(1) ㅏ : 한글 자모의 열다섯째 글자. 이름은 '아'이고 중성으로 쓴다.

The first vowel of the Korean alphabet pronounced 'a' and used as a medial.

(2) ㅑ : 한글 자모의 열여섯째 글자. 이름은 '야'이고 중성으로 쓴다.

The second vowel of the Korean alphabet pronounced 'ya' and used as a medial.

(3) ㅓ : 한글 자모의 열일곱째 글자. 이름은 '어'이고 중성으로 쓴다.

The third vowel of the Korean alphabet pronounced 'eo' and used as a middle vowel letter.

(4) ㅕ : 한글 자모의 열여덟째 글자. 이름은 '여'이고 중성으로 쓴다.

The fourth vowel of the Korean alphabet pronounced 'yeo' and used as a middle vowel letter.

(5) ㅗ : 한글 자모의 열아홉째 글자. 이름은 '오'이고 중성으로 쓴다.

The fifth vowel of the Korean alphabet pronounced 'o' and used as a middle vowel letter.

(6) ㅛ : 한글 자모의 스무째 글자. 이름은 '요'이고 중성으로 쓴다.

The sixth vowel of the Korean alphabet pronounced 'yo' and used as a middle vowel letter.

(7) ㅜ : 한글 자모의 스물한째 글자. 이름은 '우'이고 중성으로 쓴다.

The seventh vowel of the Korean alphabet pronounced 'u' and used as a middle vowel letter.

(8) ㅠ : 한글 자모의 스물두째 글자. 이름은 '유'이고 중성으로 쓴다.

The eighth vowel of the Korean alphabet pronounced 'yu' and used as a middle vowel letter.

(9) ㅡ : 한글 자모의 스물셋째 글자. 이름은 '으'이고 중성으로 쓴다.

The ninth vowel of the Korean alphabet pronounced 'eu' and used as a middle vowel letter.

(10) ㅣ : 한글 자모의 스물넷째 글자. 이름은 '이'이고 중성으로 쓴다.

The 10th vowel of the Korean alphabet pronounced ′i′ and used as a middle vowel letter.

(11) ㅚ : 한글 자모 'ㅗ'와 'ㅣ'를 모아 쓴 글자. 이름은 '외'이고 중성으로 쓴다.

The compound vowel of the Korean alphabet pronounced ′oe′, which is made by adding ′ㅣ′ to ′ㅗ′ and used as a middle vowel letter.

(12) ㅟ : 한글 자모 'ㅜ'와 'ㅣ'를 모아 쓴 글자. 이름은 '위'이고 중성으로 쓴다.

The compound vowel of the Korean alphabet pronounced ′wi′, which is made by adding ′ㅣ′ to ′ㅜ′ and used as a middle vowel letter.

(13) ㅐ : 한글 자모 'ㅏ'와 'ㅣ'를 모아 쓴 글자. 이름은 '애'이고 중성으로 쓴다.

The compound vowel of the Korean alphabet pronounced ′ae′, which is made by adding ′ㅣ′ to ′ㅏ′ and used as a medial.

(14) ㅔ : 한글 자모 'ㅓ'와 'ㅣ'를 모아 쓴 글자. 이름은 '에'이고 중성으로 쓴다.

The compound vowel of the Korean alphabet pronounced ′e′, which is made by adding ′ㅣ′ to ′ㅓ′ and used as a middle vowel letter.

(15) ㅒ : 한글 자모 'ㅑ'와 'ㅣ'를 모아 쓴 글자. 이름은 '얘'이고 중성으로 쓴다.

The compound vowel of the Korean alphabet pronounced ′yae′, which is made by adding ′ㅣ′ to ′ㅑ′ and used as a middle vowel letter.

(16) ㅖ : 한글 자모 'ㅕ'와 'ㅣ'를 모아 쓴 글자. 이름은 '예'이고 중성으로 쓴다.

The compound vowel of the Korean alphabet pronounced ′ye′, which is made by adding ′ㅣ′ to ′ㅕ′ and used as a middle vowel letter.

(17) ㅘ : 한글 자모 'ㅗ'와 'ㅏ'를 모아 쓴 글자. 이름은 '와'이고 중성으로 쓴다.

The compound vowel of the Korean alphabet pronounced ′wa′, which is made by adding ′ㅐ′ to ′ㅗ′ and used as a middle vowel letter.

(18) ㅝ : 한글 자모 'ㅜ'와 'ㅓ'를 모아 쓴 글자. 이름은 '워'이고 중성으로 쓴다.

The compound vowel of the Korean alphabet pronounced ′wo′, which is made by adding ′ㅓ′ to ′ㅜ′ and used as a middle vowel letter.

(19) ㅙ : 한글 자모 'ㅗ'와 'ㅐ'를 모아 쓴 글자. 이름은 '왜'이고 중성으로 쓴다.

The compound vowel of the Korean alphabet pronounced ´wae´, which is made by adding ´ㅐ´ to ´ㅗ´ and used as a middle vowel letter.

(20) ㅞ : 한글 자모 'ㅜ'와 'ㅔ'를 모아 쓴 글자. 이름은 '웨'이고 중성으로 쓴다.

The compound vowel of the Korean alphabet pronounced ´we´, which is made by adding ´ㅔ´ to ´ㅜ´ and used as a middle vowel letter.

(21) ㅢ : 한글 자모 'ㅡ'와 'ㅣ'를 모아 쓴 글자. 이름은 '의'이고 중성으로 쓴다.

The compound vowel of the Korean alphabet pronounced ´ui´, which is made by adding ´ㅣ´ to ´ㅡ´ and used as a middle vowel letter.

| ㅏ | ㅓ | ㅗ | ㅜ | ㅡ | ㅣ | ㅐ | ㅔ | ㅚ | ㅟ |

| ㅑ | ㅕ | ㅛ | ㅠ | ㅒ | ㅖ | ㅘ | ㅝ | ㅙ | ㅞ | ㅢ |

ㅣ + ㅏ = ㅑ   ㅣ + ㅓ = ㅕ   ㅣ + ㅗ = ㅛ   ㅣ + ㅜ = ㅠ

ㅗ + ㅏ = ㅘ   ㅜ + ㅓ = ㅝ   ㅗ + ㅐ = ㅙ   ㅜ + ㅔ = ㅞ

ㅡ + ㅣ = ㅢ

ㅏ	ㅑ	ㅓ	ㅕ	ㅗ	ㅛ	ㅜ	ㅠ	ㅡ	ㅣ
a	ya	eo	yeo	o	yo	u	yu	eu	i

ㅐ	ㅔ	ㅒ	ㅖ	ㅙ	ㅞ	ㅚ	ㅟ	ㅘ	ㅝ	ㅢ
ae	e	yae	ye	wae	we	oe	wi	wa	wo	ui

2. 자음 : 목, 입, 혀 등의 발음 기관에 의해 장애를 받으며 나는 소리.

consonant

A sound in which the air is partially or completely blocked by the movement of the throat, mouth, tongue, etc.

(1) ㄱ : 한글 자모의 첫째 글자. 이름은 기역으로 소리를 낼 때 혀뿌리가 목구멍을 막는 모양을 본떠 만든 글자이다.

The first consonant of the Korean alphabet pronounced giyeok, the sound of which is created by imitating the root of one′s tongue blocking one′s throat.

(2) ㄴ : 한글 자모의 둘째 글자. 이름은 ‘니은’으로 소리를 낼 때 혀끝이 윗잇몸에 붙는 모양을 본떠 만든 글자이다.

The second consonant of the Korean alphabet pronounced nieun, the sound of which is created by imitating the tip of the tongue reaching the upper gum.

(3) ㄷ : 한글 자모의 셋째 글자. 이름은 ‘디귿’으로, 소리를 낼 때 혀의 모습은 ‘ㄴ’과 같지만 더 세게 발음 되므로 한 획을 더해 만든 글자이다.

The third consonant of the Korean alphabet pronounced digeut, which is made by adding a stroke to ′ㄴ′, as the tongue looks the same as that of ′ㄴ′ but ′ㄷ′ is pronounced more strongly.

(4) ㄹ : 한글 자모의 넷째 글자. 이름은 ‘리을’로 혀끝을 윗잇몸에 가볍게 대었다가 떼면서 내는 소리를 나타낸다.

The fourth consonant in the Korean alphabet pronounced rieul, the sound of which is created by lightly touching the tip of the tongue to the upper gum and then lowering it.

(5) ㅁ : 한글 자모의 다섯째 글자. 이름은 ‘미음’으로, 소리를 낼 때 다물어지는 두 입술 모양을 본떠서 만든 글자이다.

The fifth consonant of the Korean alphabet pronounced mieum, the sound of which is created by imitating the closed shape of the lips.

(6) ㅂ : 한글 자모의 여섯째 글자. 이름은 ‘비읍’으로, 소리를 낼 때의 입술 모양은 ‘ㅁ’과 같지만 더 세게 발음되므로 ‘ㅁ’에 획을 더해서 만든 글자이다.

The sixth consonant of the Korean alphabet pronounced bieup, which is made by adding strokes to ′ㅁ′, as the lips look the same as those of ′ㅁ′ but ′ㅂ′ is pronounced more strongly.

(7) ㅅ : 한글 자모의 일곱째 글자. 이름은 '시옷'으로 이의 모양을 본떠서 만든 글자이다.

The seventh consonant of the Korean alphabet pronounced siot, the sound of which is created by imitating the shape of teeth.

(8) ㅇ : 한글 자모의 여덟째 글자. 이름은 '이응'으로 목구멍의 모양을 본떠서 만든 글자이다. 초성으로 쓰일 때 소리가 없다.

The eighth consonant of the Korean alphabet pronounced ieung or not pronounced at all when used as the first consonant letter, the sound of which is created by imitating the shape of a throat.

(9) ㅈ : 한글 자모의 아홉째 글자. 이름은 '지읒'으로, 'ㅅ'보다 소리가 더 세게 나므로 'ㅅ'에 한 획을 더해 만든 글자이다.

The ninth consonant of the Korean alphabet pronounced jieut, which is made by adding a stroke to ´ㅅ´, as the tongue is shaped the same as that of ´ㅅ´ but ´ㅈ´ is pronounced more strongly.

(10) ㅊ : 한글 자모의 열째 글자. 이름은 '치읓'으로 '지읒'보다 소리가 거세게 나므로 '지읒'에 한 획을 더 해서 만든 글자이다.

The 10th consonant of the Korean alphabet pronounced chieut, which is made by adding a stroke to ´ㅈ´, as it is pronounced more strongly than ´ㅈ.´

(11) ㅋ : 한글 자모의 열한째 글자. 이름은 '키읔'으로 'ㄱ'보다 소리가 거세게 나므로 'ㄱ'에 한 획을 더 하여 만든 글자이다.

The 11th consonant of the Korean alphabet pronounced kieuk, which is made by adding a stroke to ´ㄱ´, as it is pronounced more strongly than ´ㄱ.´

(12) ㅌ : 한글 자모의 열두째 글자. 이름은 '티읕'으로, 'ㄷ'보다 소리가 거세게 나므로 'ㄷ'에 한 획을 더 하여 만든 글자이다.

The 12th consonant of the Korean alphabet pronounced tieut, which is made by adding a stroke to ´ㄷ´, as it is pronounced more strongly than ´ㄷ.´

(13) ㅍ : 한글 자모의 열셋째 글자. 이름은 '피읖'으로, 'ㅁ, ㅂ'보다 소리가 거세게 나므로 'ㅁ'에 획을 더 하여 만든 글자이다.

The 13th consonant of the Korean alphabet pronounced pieup, which is made by adding a stroke to ´ㅁ´, as it is pronounced more strongly than ´ㅁ´ and ´ㅂ.´

(14) ㅎ : 한글 자모의 열넷째 글자. 이름은 '히읗'으로, 이 글자의 소리는 목청에서 나므로 목구멍을 본떠 만든 'ㅇ'의 경우와 같지만 'ㅇ'보다 더 세게 나므로 'ㅇ'에 획을 더하여 만든 글자이다.

The 14th consonant of the Korean alphabet pronounced hieut, which is made by adding a stroke to 'ㅇ', as its sound comes from one's vocal cords like 'ㅇ,' which is created by imitating the shape of a throat, but pronounced more strongly than 'ㅇ.'

(15) ㄲ : 한글 자모 'ㄱ'을 겹쳐 쓴 글자. 이름은 쌍기역으로, 'ㄱ'의 된소리이다.

The consonant in the Korean alphabet consisting of two 'ㄱ' which creates a stronger sound than a single 'ㄱ'.

(16) ㄸ : 한글 자모 'ㄷ'을 겹쳐 쓴 글자. 이름은 쌍디귿으로, 'ㄷ'의 된소리이다.

The consonant in the Korean alphabet consisting of two 'ㄷ' which creates a stronger sound than a single 'ㄷ'.

(17) ㅃ : 한글 자모 'ㅂ'을 겹쳐 쓴 글자. 이름은 쌍비읍으로, 'ㅂ'의 된소리이다.

The consonant of the Korean alphabet consisting of two 'ㅂ' which creates a stronger sound than a single 'ㅂ'.

(18) ㅆ : 한글 자모 'ㅅ'을 겹쳐 쓴 글자. 이름은 쌍시옷으로, 'ㅅ'의 된소리이다.

The consonant in the Korean alphabet consisting of two 'ㅅ', which is called double siot and which creates a stronger sound than a single 'ㅅ'.

(19) ㅉ : 한글 자모 'ㅈ'을 겹쳐 쓴 글자. 이름은 쌍지읒으로, 'ㅈ'의 된소리이다.

The consonant in the Korean alphabet consisting of two 'ㅈ' which creates a stronger sound than a single 'ㅈ'.

ㄱ	ㄴ	ㄷ	ㄹ	ㅁ	ㅂ	ㅅ	ㅇ	ㅈ	ㅊ	ㅋ	ㅌ	ㅍ	ㅎ
g,k	n	d,t	r,l	m	b,p	s	ng	j	ch	k	t	p	h

ㄲ	ㄸ	ㅃ	ㅆ	ㅉ
kk	tt	pp	ss	jj

ㄱ	ㄴ	ㄷ	ㄹ	ㅁ	ㅂ	ㅅ	ㅇ	ㅈ		ㅎ
ㅋ		ㅌ			ㅍ			ㅊ		
ㄲ		ㄸ			ㅃ	ㅆ		ㅉ		

3. 음절 : 모음, 모음과 자음, 자음과 모음, 자음과 모음과 자음이 어울려 한 덩어리로 내는 말소리의 단위.

syllable
The unit of a speech that is pronounced as one lump, which includes a vowel, the combination of a vowel and a consonant, the combination of a consonant and a vowel, and the combination of a consonant, a vowel, and a consonant.

1) 모음(vowel)

   예 (example) : 아, 어, 오, 우……

2) 자음(consonant) + 모음(vowel)

   예 (example) : 가, 도, 루, 슈……

3) 모음(vowel) + 자음(consonant)

   예 (example) : 악, 얌, 임, 윤……

4) 자음(consonant) + 모음(vowel) + 자음(consonant)

   예 (example) : 각, 남, 당, 균……

	ㄱ	ㄴ	ㄷ	ㄹ	ㅁ	ㅂ	ㅅ	ㅇ	ㅈ	ㅊ	ㅋ	ㅌ	ㅍ	ㅎ
ㅏ	가	나	다	라	마	바	사	아	자	차	카	타	파	하
ㅓ	거	너	더	러	머	버	서	어	저	처	커	터	퍼	허
ㅗ	고	노	도	로	모	보	소	오	조	초	코	토	포	호
ㅜ	구	누	두	루	무	부	수	우	주	추	쿠	투	푸	후
ㅡ	그	느	드	르	므	브	스	으	즈	츠	크	트	프	흐
ㅣ	기	니	디	리	미	비	시	이	지	치	키	티	피	히
ㅐ	개	내	대	래	매	배	새	애	재	채	캐	태	패	해
ㅔ	게	네	데	레	메	베	세	에	제	체	케	테	페	헤
ㅚ	괴	뇌	되	뢰	뫼	뵈	쇠	외	죄	최	쾨	퇴	푀	회
ㅟ	귀	뉘	뒤	뤼	뮈	뷔	쉬	위	쥐	취	퀴	튀	퓌	휘
ㅑ	갸	냐	댜	랴	먀	뱌	샤	야	쟈	챠	캬	탸	퍄	햐
ㅕ	겨	녀	뎌	려	며	벼	셔	여	져	쳐	켜	텨	펴	혀
ㅛ	교	뇨	됴	료	묘	뵤	쇼	요	죠	쵸	쿄	툐	표	효
ㅠ	규	뉴	듀	류	뮤	뷰	슈	유	쥬	츄	큐	튜	퓨	휴
ㅒ	걔	냬	댸	럐	먜	뱨	섀	얘	쟤	챘	걔	턔	퍠	햬
ㅖ	계	녜	뎨	례	몌	볘	셰	예	졔	쳬	켸	톄	폐	혜
ㅘ	과	놔	돠	롸	뫄	봐	솨	와	좌	촤	콰	톼	퐈	화
ㅝ	궈	눠	둬	뤄	뭐	붜	숴	워	줘	춰	쿼	퉈	풔	훠
ㅙ	괘	놰	돼	뢔	뫠	봬	쇄	왜	좨	쵀	쾌	퇘	퐤	홰
ㅞ	궤	눼	뒈	뤠	뭬	붸	쉐	웨	줴	췌	퀘	퉤	풰	훼
ㅢ	긔	늬	듸	릐	믜	븨	싀	의	즤	츼	킈	틔	픠	희

4. 품사 : 단어를 기능, 형태, 의미에 따라 나눈 갈래.

part of speech
Words divided by their functions, forms, and meanings.

• **체언** : 문장에서 명사, 대명사, 수사와 같이 문장의 주어나 목적어 등의 기능을 하는 말.

substantive
A word such as a noun, pronoun, and numeral which functions as the subject, object, etc., of a sentence.

• **용언** : 문법에서, 동사나 형용사와 같이 문장에서 서술어의 기능을 하는 말.

predicate
In grammar, a word such as a verb or adjective which functions as a predicate in a sentence.

1) **본용언** : 문장의 주체를 주되게 서술하면서 보조 용언의 도움을 받는 용언.

main predicate element
A predicate that mainly describes the subject of a sentence, assisted by an auxiliary predicate element.

2) **보조 용언** : 본용언과 연결되어 그 뜻을 보충해 주는 용언.

auxiliary predicate element
A predicate element that conjoins with the main part of the predicate to complement its meaning.

• **수식언** : 문법에서, 관형어나 부사어와 같이 뒤에 오는 체언이나 용언을 꾸미거나 한정하는 말.

modifier
A sentence component such as an adnominal phrase or adverb that modifies or qualifies following substantives or predicates.

---

1. **명사** : 사물의 이름을 나타내는 품사.

noun
A part of speech that indicates a person, place or thing.

2. **대명사** : 다른 명사를 대신하여 사람, 장소, 사물 등을 가리키는 낱말.

pronoun
A word that substitutes for a noun referring to a person, place, object, etc.

3. 수사 : 수량이나 순서를 나타내는 말.

numeral

A word that expresses the amount or order of something.

4. 동사 : 사람이나 사물의 움직임을 나타내는 품사.

verb

A part of speech that expresses the movement of a person or thing.

5. 형용사 : 사람이나 사물의 성질이나 상태를 나타내는 품사.

adjective

A part of speech that shows the quality or state of a person or thing.

• 활용 : 문법적 관계를 나타내기 위해 용언의 꼴을 조금 바꿈.

conjugation

An act of slightly changing the form of a predicate to indicate grammatical relations.

1) 규칙 활용 : 문법에서, 동사나 형용사가 활용을 할 때 어간의 형태가 변하지 않고 일반적인 어미가 붙어 변화하는 것.

regular conjugation

In grammar, inflection of a verb or adjective in which its root stays unchanged while regular word endings are attached to the root.

2) 불규칙 활용 : 문법에서, 동사나 형용사가 활용을 할 때 어간의 형태가 변하거나 예외적인 어미가 붙어 변화하는 것.

irregular conjugation

A grammatical inflection of a verb or adjective in which its root changes or irregular verbal endings are attached to the root.

활용(conjugation) 형태(form)	어간(stem) + 어미(ending of a word)	불규칙(irregularity) 부분(part)	불규칙 용언(irregular predicate element)
물어	묻- + -어	묻- → 물-	싣다, 붇다, 일컫다…
지어	짓- + -어	짓- → 지-	젓다, 붓다, 잇다…
누워	눕- + -어	눕- → 누우	줍다, 굽다, 깁다…
흘러	흐르- + -어	흐르- → 흘ㄹ	부르다, 타오르다, 누르다…
하얘	하양- + -아	-양어- → 애	빨갛다, 까맣다, 뽀얗다…

1) **어간** : 동사나 형용사가 활용할 때에 변하지 않는 부분.

stem; base
The part of a word that remains the same after the conjugation of the verb or adjective.

2) **어미** : 용언이나 '-이다'에서 활용할 때 형태가 달라지는 부분.

ending of a word
The part that changes in a predicate or predicative particle ´이다´ (be) when it undergoes an conjugation.

① **어말 어미** : 동사, 형용사, 서술격 조사가 활용될 때 맨 뒤에 오는 어미.

final ending
An ending of a word that comes last when a verb, adjective, or predicative particle is conjugated.

㉠ **종결 어미** : 한 문장을 끝맺는 기능을 하는 어말 어미.

sentence-closing ending
An ending that is used to finish a sentence.

㉡ **전성 어미** : 동사나 형용사의 어간에 붙어 동사나 형용사가 명사, 관형사, 부사와 같은 다른 품사의 기능을 가지도록 하는 어미.

transformative ending
An ending that is attached to the stem of a verb or adjective and changes it into a different part of speech such as noun, determiner or adverb.

㉢ **연결 어미** : 어간에 붙어 다음 말에 연결하는 기능을 하는 어미.

connective ending
The ending of a word that connects to the next word, by being attached to the stem.

② **선어말 어미** : 어말 어미 앞에 놓여 높임이나 시제 등을 나타내는 어미.

pre-final ending
An ending of a word inserted between the stem of a verb and a final ending, which indicates honorifics, tense, etc.

어미 (ending of a word)			형태 (form)	
어말 어미 (final ending)	종결 어미 (sentence-closing ending)	평서형 (declarative form)	-다, -네, -ㅂ니다/습니다…	
		의문형 (interrogative mood)	-는가, -니, -ㄹ까…	
		감탄형 (exclamatory form)	-구나, -네…	
		명령형 (imperative mood)	-(으)세요, -어라/-아라/-여라	
		청유형 (conjugated form of request)	-자, -ㅂ시다/-읍시다, -세…	
	연결 어미 (connective ending)		-고, -며/으며, -지만, -거나, -어서, -려고/-으려고, -면/-으면…	
	전성 어미 (transformative ending)	명사형 어미 (nominal ending)	-ㅁ/-음, -기	
		관형사형 어미 (adnominal suffix)	과거 (past tense)	-ㄴ/-은
			현재 (present)	-는
			미래 (future)	-ㄹ/-을
			중단/반복 (suspension/repetition)	-던
		부사형 어미 (adverbial ending)	-게, -도록, -듯이, -이	
선어말 어미 (pre-final ending)	주체(agent) 높임(honorific)		-시-/-으시-	
	시제 (tense)		과거 (past tense)	-았-/-었-/-였-
			현재 (present)	-ㄴ-/-는-
			미래 (future)	-ㄹ-/-을-
			회상 (reflection)	-더-

6. **관형사** : 체언 앞에 쓰여 그 체언의 내용을 꾸며 주는 기능을 하는 말.

determiner

A word used in front of a substantive, whose function is to modify the substantive.

7. **부사** : 주로 동사나 형용사 앞에 쓰여 그 뜻을 분명하게 하는 말.

adverb

A word that usually occurs before a verb or an adjective and specifies their meaning.

8. **조사** : 명사, 대명사, 수사, 부사, 어미 등에 붙어 그 말과 다른 말과의 문법적 관계를 표시하거나 그 말의 뜻을 도와주는 품사.

postpositional particle; postpositional marker

A part of speech that is attached behind a noun, pronoun, numeral, adverb, ending, etc., to indicate its grammatical relationship to the clause or make it more specific in meaning.

1) **격 조사** : 명사나 명사구 뒤에 붙어 그 말이 서술어에 대하여 가지는 문법적 관계를 나타내는 조사.

case-marking postpositional particle

A postpositional particle attached to a noun or noun phrase, which indicates their grammatical status in relation to the predicate.

① **주격 조사** : 문장에서 서술어에 대한 주어의 자격을 표시하는 조사.

subject case marker

A postpositional word to indicate the qualification of a subject for a predicate in a sentence.

② **목적격 조사** : 문장에서 서술어에 대한 목적어의 자격을 표시하는 조사.

object case marker

A postpositional particle that indicates the grammatical status of the object with regard to the predicate in a sentence.

③ **서술격 조사** : 문장 안에서 체언이나 체언 구실을 하는 말 뒤에 붙어 이들을 서술어로 만드는 격 조사.

predicative particle

A case-marking postpositional particle attached to a substantive or a word acting as a substantive, and make it function as a predicate in a sentence.

④ **보격 조사** : 문장 안에서, 체언이 서술어의 보어임을 표시하는 격 조사.

complement case marker
In a sentence, the case-marking postpositional particle that indicates that the substantive is the complement to the predicate.

⑤ **관형격 조사** : 문장 안에서 앞에 오는 체언이 뒤에 오는 체언을 꾸며 주는 구실을 하게 하는 조사.

adnominal case marker
A postpositional particle enabling a substantive to qualify another substantive immediately following it in a sentence.

⑥ **부사격 조사** : 문장 안에서, 체언이 서술어에 대하여 장소, 도구, 자격, 원인, 시간 등과 같은 부사로서의 자격을 가지게 하는 조사.

adverbial case marker
A postpositional particle attached to a substantive, which transforms the substantive into an adverb indicating a place, tool, qualification, cause, time, etc., in relation to the predicate.

⑦ **호격 조사** : 문장에서 체언이 독립적으로 쓰여 부르는 말의 역할을 하게 하는 조사.

vocative case marker
A postpositional particle that enables a substantive used independently in a sentence to refer to the person or thing being addressed.

2) **보조사** : 체언, 부사, 활용 어미 등에 붙어서 특별한 의미를 더해 주는 조사.

auxiliary postpositional particle
A postpositional particle that is attached to a substantive, adverb, conjugational verbal ending, etc., to add a special meaning to the word.

3) **접속 조사** : 두 단어를 이어 주는 기능을 하는 조사.

conjunctive postpositional particle
A postpositional particle that connects two words.

	주격 조사 (subject case marker)	이/가, 께서, 에서
격 조사 (case-marking postpositional particle)	목적격 조사 (object case marker)	을/를
	보격 조사 (complement case marker)	이/가
	부사격 조사 (adverbial case marker)	에, 에서, 에게, 한테, 께, (으)로, (으)로서, (으)로써, 와/과, 하고, (이)랑, 처럼, 만큼, 같이, 보다
	관형격 조사 (adnominal case marker)	의
	서술격 조사 (predicative particle)	이다
	호격 조사 (vocative case marker)	아, 야, 이시여
보조사 (auxiliary postpositional particle)		은/는, 만, 도, 까지, 부터, 마저, 조차, 밖에…
접속 조사 (conjunctive postpositional particle)		와/과, 하고, (이)랑, (이)며

9. **감탄사** : 느낌이나 부름, 응답 등을 나타내는 말의 품사.

interjection
A part of speech referring to a word that expresses a feeling, an act of calling or responding, etc.

5. 문장 성분 : 주어, 서술어, 목적어 등과 같이 한 문장을 구성하는 요소.

sentence component
An element that constitutes a sentence such as a subject, predicate, object, etc.

1. 주어 : 문장의 주요 성분의 하나로, 주로 문장의 앞에 나와서 동작이나 상태의 주체가 되는 말.

subject
A major sentence component that mainly comes at the beginning of a sentence and serves as the agent of an action or state.

1) 체언 + 주격 조사 : substantive + subject case marker

2) 체언 + 보조사 : substantive + auxiliary postpositional particle

2. 목적어 : 타동사가 쓰인 문장에서 동작의 대상이 되는 말.

object
A word that is the target of an action in a sentence with a transitive verb.

1) 체언 + 목적격 조사 : substantive + object case marker

2) 체언 + 보조사 : substantive + auxiliary postpositional particle

3. 서술어 : 문장에서 주어의 성질, 상태, 움직임 등을 나타내는 말.

predicate
A word that shows the subject's character, state, movement, etc., in a sentence.

1) 용언 종결형 : predicate sentence-closing conjugation

2) 체언 + 서술격 조사 '이다' : substantive + predicative particle '이다'

4. 보어 : 주어와 서술어만으로는 뜻이 완전하지 못할 때 보충하여 문장의 뜻을 완전하게 하는 문장 성분.

complement
A sentence component that completes the meaning of a sentence when the subject and the predicate alone do not constitute a complete meaning.

1) 체언 + 보격 조사 : substantive + complement case marker

2) 체언 + 보조사 : substantive + auxiliary postpositional particle

5. **관형어** : 체언 앞에서 그 내용을 꾸며 주는 문장 성분.

adnominal phrase
A sentence component that modifies a substantive following it.

1) 관형사 : determiner

2) 체언 + 관형격 조사 '의' : substantive + adnominal case marker '의'

3) 용언 어간 + 관형사형 어미 '-은/ㄴ, -는, -을/ㄹ, -던'

    : predicate stem + adnominal suffix '-은/ㄴ, -는, -을/ㄹ, -던'

6. **부사어** : 문장 안에서, 용언의 뜻을 분명하게 하는 문장 성분.

adverb
A sentence component that specifies the meaning of the predicate in a sentence.

1) 부사 : adverb

2) 부사 + 보조사 : adverb + auxiliary postpositional particle

3) 용언 어간 + 부사형 어미 '-게' : predicate stem + adverbial ending '-게'

7. **독립어** : 문장의 다른 성분과 밀접한 관계없이 독립적으로 쓰는 말.

independent word
A word used independently without any relation to other constituents in a sentence.

1) 감탄사 : interjection

2) 체언 + 호격 조사 : substantive + vocative case marker

6. 어순 : 한 문장 안에서 주어, 목적어, 서술어 등의 문장 성분이 나오는 순서.

order of words

The order in which the sentence components such as subject, object and predicate are arranged within a sentence.

1) 주어 + 서술어(자동사)

   subject + predicate(intransitive verb)

   예 (example) : 바람이 불어요.

2) 주어 + 서술어(형용사)

   subject + predicate(adjective)

   예 (example) : 날씨가 좋아요.

3) 주어 + 서술어(체언+서술격 조사 '이다')

   subject + predicate(substantive+predicative particle '이다')

   예 (example) : 이것이 책상이다.

4) 주어 + 목적어 + 서술어(타동사)

   subject + object + predicate(transitive verb)

   예 (example) : 친구가 밥을 먹어요.

5) 주어 + 목적어 + 필수 부사어 + 서술어(타동사)

   subject + object + essentials adverb + predicate(transitive verb)

   예 (example) : 어머니께서 용돈을 나에게 주셨다.

1) <u>체언(명사/대명사/수사)이/가</u>   +   <u>형용사 어간어미</u>
   　　　<주어>　　　　　　　　　　<서술어>

2) <u>체언이/가</u>   +   <u>체언을/를</u>   +   <u>타동사 어간어미</u>
   　　<주어>　　　　　<목적어>　　　　　<서술어>

1) <u>체언(명사/대명사/수사)이/가</u>   +   <u>형용사 어간어미</u>

7. 띄어쓰기 : 글을 쓸 때, 각 낱말마다 띄어서 쓰는 일. 또는 그것에 관한 규칙.

word spacing
The act of separating words by the insertion of spaces when writing, or the rules on such spacing.

1) 체언조사 (띄어쓰기) 용언 어간어미

substantivepostpositional particle (word spacing) predicate stemending of a word

예 (example) : 밥을 (word spacing) 먹어요

2) 관형사 (띄어쓰기) 명사

determiner (word spacing) noun

예 (example) : 새 (word spacing) 옷

3) 용언 어간관형사형 어미 '-은/-ㄴ, -는, -을/-ㄹ, -던' (띄어쓰기) 명사

predicate stemadnominal suffix '-은/-ㄴ, -는, -을/-ㄹ, -던 (word spacing) noun

예 (example) : 기다리는 (word spacing) 사람 / 좋은 (word spacing) 사람

4) 형용사 어간부사형 어미 '-게' (띄어쓰기) 용언 어간어미

adjective stemadverbial ending '-게' (word spacing) predicate stemending of a word

예 (example) : 행복하게 (word spacing) 살자

5) 명사인 (띄어쓰기) 명사

noun인 (word spacing) noun

예 (example) : 대학생인 (word spacing) 친구

8. 문장 부호 : 문장의 뜻을 정확히 전달하고, 문장을 읽고 이해하기 쉽도록 쓰는 부호.

punctuation
A mark used to convey the meaning of a sentence clearly, or to make it easier to be read and understood.

1) 마침표 (.) : 문장을 끝맺거나 연월일을 표시하거나 특정한 의미가 있는 날을 표시하거나 장, 절, 항 등을 표시하는 문자나 숫자 다음에 쓰는 문장 부호.

period; full stop
A punctuation mark used to end a sentence, indicate a year, month or day, indicate a special day, or put after a letter or number indicating a chapter, passage, clause, etc.

2) 물음표 (?) : 의심이나 의문을 나타내거나 적절한 말을 쓰기 어렵거나 모르는 내용임을 나타낼 때 쓰는 문장 부호.

question mark
A punctuation mark used to express doubt or interrogation, used when it is difficult to choose the appropriate words or when one does not know.

3) 느낌표 (!) : 강한 느낌을 표현할 때 문장 마지막에 쓰는 문장 부호 '!'의 이름.

exclamation mark
A name for the punctuation mark '!' which, coming at the end of a sentence, expresses emphatic feelings.

4) 쉼표 (,) : 어구를 나열하거나 문장의 연결 관계를 나타내는 문장 부호.

comma
A punctuation mark used to list words or phrases or show the connection between sentences.

5) 줄임표 (……) : 할 말을 줄였을 때나 말이 없음을 나타낼 때에 쓰는 문장 부호.

ellipsis
A punctuation mark used to indicate a shortening or omission of words.

< 참고 문헌 (reference) >

고려대학교 한국어대사전, 고려대학교 민족문화연구원, 2009
우리말샘, 국립국어원, 2016
표준국어대사전, 국립국어원, 1999
한국어교육 문법 자료편, 한글파크, 2016
한국어 교육학 사전, 하우, 2014
한국어기초사전, 국립국어원, 2016
한국어 문법 총론 Ⅰ, 집문당, 2015

HANPUK

한국어 동사 290 형용사 137 English(translation)

발　행 | 2024년 6월 11일
저　자 | 주식회사 한글2119연구소
펴낸이 | 한건희
펴낸곳 | 주식회사 부크크
출판사등록 | 2014.07.15.(제2014-16호)
주　소 | 서울특별시 금천구 가산디지털1로 119 SK트윈타워 A동 305호
전　화 | 1670-8316
이메일 | info@bookk.co.kr

ISBN | 979-11-410-8883-5

www.bookk.co.kr